THE THOU

THE THOUGHT OF GOD

*

MAURICE ROBERTS

THE BANNER OF TRUTH TRUST

THE BANNER OF TRUTH TRUST
3 Murrayfield Road, Edinburgh EH12 6EL
P.O. Box 621, Carlisle, Pennsylvania 17013, USA

*

© Maurice Roberts 1993
First Published 1993
Reprinted 1995
ISBN 0 85151 658 0

*

Typeset in 11¹/₂/13pt Garamond Monotype
Printed and bound in Great Britain by
BPC Paperbacks Ltd
a member of
The British Printing Company Ltd

TO
MY MOTHER
AND TO THE MEMORY OF
MY FATHER —
BOTH CHRISTIANS

Contents

Preface

To those who know of him, the name of Maurice Roberts will signify different things: to some he is chiefly known as the minister of the congregation of the Free Church of Scotland in Ayr, in the south-west of Scotland. To a wider circle in the United Kingdom, and increasingly beyond, he has come to be appreciated for his preaching ministry at conferences and in other contacts. But since 1988 he has served a yet more wide-spread and scattered circle as Editor of the Trust's monthly magazine, *The Banner of Truth*.

In addition to the learning of a theologian, the instincts of a pastor, the experience of a former classics teacher and his gifts as an editor, he has enhanced the pages of the magazine with his own regular editorial articles. These essays have been widely read and appreciated. Pointedly biblical, they are thoughtful and searching, humbling and exalting, challenging and encouraging.

Like editorials in other journals, Maurice Roberts' articles have spoken to the needs of the times. But many editorials appear to have only historical or sociological interest at a later date. By contrast, these are of lasting value. They have God and his Word as their starting place; their horizon stretches beyond time to eternity. Those who have already read them will rejoice to have them conveniently and permanently in book form, while those who come to them for the first time will appreciate their

freshness, relevance and power, and will find in them a seriousness which has a sanctifying effect on the heart and a clarifying
influence on the spiritual vision. The publishers believe that
many who possess *The Thought of God* will turn to it again and
again for spiritual help.

The death of thought in the western world has caused general
and widespread alarm. Nor can evangelical Christianity escape
the charge of sharing the contemporary world's preference for
feeling rather than *thinking*. By contrast, in biblical teaching only
right thinking about God is capable of producing right feeling
about anything. It is the apostle Paul who teaches us that sanctified emotions and transformed lives are the fruit of renewed
minds (*Rom.* 12:1-2). No reader of these essays will be left in any
doubt about the powerful effect of such renewal. Those who
come to these pages thoughtfully and prayerfully, in the presence
of God, will close them as wiser, humbler and, please God,
holier and more joyful men and women than when they opened
them.

The Publishers,
Edinburgh,
August 1993.

I

Our Great God

Great is the Lord,
and greatly to be praised;
and his greatness is unsearchable . . .
I will speak of the glorious
honour of thy majesty,
and of thy wondrous works.

Psalm 145:3, 5.

1

The Thought of God

It is very clear from Scripture that good men do, and evil men do not, turn intuitively to God when confronted with troubles. When, for instance, David's followers for once turned against him after the sacking of Ziklag and were so upset at the loss of wife and children that they were near to stoning him, we are informed that 'David encouraged himself in the Lord his God' [1 Sam. 30:6]. Similarly, when Sennacherib and Rabshakeh laid siege to Jerusalem and all earthly hope of deliverance was cut off, Hezekiah, we are told, 'spread it before the Lord' [2 Kings 19:14]. Again, when Nehemiah had betrayed his secret concern for God's cause to Artaxerxes by an involuntary facial expression and was invited to make plain his request, he tells us that he 'prayed to the God of heaven' [Neh. 2:4]. Like a flash of lightning, the souls of good men turn upwards to God when trials and fears confront them.

Whole psalms appear to have been written very largely for the purpose of encouraging believers to think of God when calamity strikes or when perplexity overshadows them. 'I will not be afraid of ten thousands' [Ps. 3:6], affirms David, when his enemies are increased. 'I will call upon the Lord, who is worthy to be praised: so shall I be saved from mine enemies' [Ps. 18:3]. 'The Lord is my light and my salvation; whom shall I fear?'

[*Ps.* 27:1]. 'I cried unto thee, and thou hast healed me' [*Ps.* 30:2]. 'I sought the Lord, and he heard me, and delivered me from all my fears' [*Ps.* 34:4]. 'He is their strength in the time of trouble' [*Ps.* 37:39]. 'God is our refuge and strength, a very present help in trouble' [*Ps.* 46:1]. These and scores of similar passages in the psalms reassure us that godly men are not more ready to raise their minds to God in trouble than he is to hear and help them. Indeed, the whole Bible sets this truth before us.

On the other hand, the unconverted have no spiritual access to God in the time of distress but are commonly swallowed up with despair like Saul and Judas; or else they harden themselves against God, like Pharaoh, till they become reckless. Afflictions, therefore, are a fan in God's hand to separate between good and evil men. All men are good company in fair weather but the storms of life prove spiritual character. In trouble, where do our thoughts fly to? To 'curse God and die' is the essential and inevitable philosophy of graceless men when they are surprised by sudden calamity. But the child of God instinctively looks at life's miseries with a theological eye and finds God to be a comfort when all seems as bad as it can be: 'Though he slay me, yet will I trust in him' [*Job* 13:15].

To have God in his mind and thought is the believer's constant source of strength. The martyr languishes in the flames but his mind flies upward to God his Saviour and looks forward blissfully to the glory that awaits him even as his body sinks to ashes. The imprisoned Christian forgets the harsh regime of the camp, the daily grind and gruelling labour, as his mind soars upward on the wings of hope to remember God. The weary missionary, struggling with unfamiliar syllables and convoluted grammar in his appointed sphere of service sees beyond the frustrations of the hour as he remembers God, his 'exceeding great reward' [*Gen.* 15:1]. The faithful pastor of a congregation, entombed in his study and confronted with an impossible daily agenda of duties, brightens in his heart and feels his pulse quicken as he remembers his Master above. The thought of God enlivens all action.

The thought of God should be the Christian's panacea. It should cure all his ills at a stroke. And what an infinity there is in the thought of God! Nothing can approach in beauty to the idea of the true and living God. That there exists a Being who is infinite in power, knowledge and goodness, that that Being cares for me with a perfect love as though I were the only man in existence, that he loved me before I was born and created me to enjoy him eternally and that he sent his Son to suffer the agony of the cross to secure my eternal happiness—that, surely, must be a thought to end all sorrow. It ought to be and often it is.

There is a difference, alas, between things as they are and things as we perceive them. Our perceptions of God suffer more than our perceptions of natural things because we are depraved and do not make it our life's work daily to enrich our idea of God from the fountainhead of Scripture. It is our folly that we allow ourselves to look at life's problems as if they were somehow isolated from God. As soon as we see our problems in the light of God's Being and perfection, we are emancipated from alarm and terror. It therefore remains a principle of universal application that we can cope with our afflictions just so long as we 'look not at the things which are seen, but at the things which are not seen' [*2 Cor.* 4:18]. It is this habit of mind which the Scriptures call 'faith' and which they praise in Moses when they inform us that 'he endured as seeing him who is invisible', that is, God [*Heb.* 11:27].

This eleventh chapter of Hebrews, indeed, has a good deal to teach us about the subject in hand. For, what was it that inspired the patriarchs, heroes and saints in that chapter to do their great exploits, except the mental image which they continually held of God as the God who 'is and is a rewarder of them that diligently seek him' [*Heb.* 11:6]? It might truly be said of them that they laboured and suffered, one and all, for one reason only, that God was ever present to their mind's eye. To this one explanation may be traced all their voluntary exertions and discomforts, that they had God constantly in the foreground of their thought. And those who think of God as he truly is know that it is a good exchange to lose home and country, family and fortune, health and comfort—yes, and life itself—to gain possession of God himself in the end.

The art of good thinking is to carry thought to its logical conclusion. Sir Isaac Newton is said to have claimed no more for his profound theories than that he took the lines of his thought farther than other men did and so perceived the hidden 'laws' which he formulated. That is a lesson which Christians can learn from. The mere thought of God should end all anxiety. Then why in my case does it not? Because I fail to carry thought to its proper conclusion.

If God be God, then no insoluble problems exist. And if God be *my* God, then no problem of mine is without its appropriate solution. There is in God just exactly what is needed to solve every riddle of life. Such a Being is God that he comprehends in himself all that we could ever need to neutralize all evils, veto all temptations, negative all sorrows and compensate for all losses. More still, there is in God such a supply of competence and wisdom that he is able to transform every ill into good as soon as it touches us. God has, so to say, the 'Midas touch', by which all the Christian's problems turn to gold in his hands. To be told that 'all things work together for good' [*Rom.* 8:28] to us is to have more than a cordial. It is to have the elixir of life.

Panic is the sinful failure to apply our knowledge of God to particular problems. Peter looks at the waves and begins to sink. The disciples in the boat are alarmed at the storm. Like them, we also fall into periodic fits of despair at the state of society, the state of the church, the state of the mission-field where we serve perhaps, or else at the imperfect state of our own souls. Panic is possible only when God is obscured from our thoughts by visible circumstances.

It must follow from what has been said that the degree of a Christian's peace of mind depends upon his spiritual ability to interpose the thought of God between himself and his anxiety. When the dark cloud of trouble first looms up on the horizon of our thought, then is the time to apply our theology in downright earnest. For it is not outward circumstances that can drag us down, but our own reaction of despair to them, when we fail to perceive the hidden hand of God in all events.

There is no situation in life too hard for God. But many situations look too hard at first sight. These are ordained to give us room to wait on God for his deliverance. There is a blessing attached to waiting patiently on God in evil days. The impatient urge to resign and run away when times are trying is unworthy of the sons of God. There is a better way. Let us remember God and take fresh courage. He who believes shall not make haste and, conversely, they shall not be ashamed who wait for God [*Isa.* 28:16; 49:23].

It is instinctive for the Christian in every time of fear or trouble to turn to thoughts of God. To the unspiritual mind this is contemptible escapism, a mere 'opium of the people'. But in reality it is an activity of faith and worship and one which is highly pleasing to God. If God indeed were only a mental fiction, there would be nothing more to commend the practice of devout meditation on his excellence and glory than that it was pious optimism, wishful thinking which benefits the mind just so much as 'positive thinking' is said to do and no more. Since, however, God exists in reality and is not a spiritual medicine invented by our fears, it must follow that life's secret very largely consists in holding him in our thoughts as much as possible and especially in times of fear and need.

2
'O The Depth!'

Perhaps the greatest disservice done to the Christian religion in the past hundred years by churches in the western world has been to trivialize it. This sin has always been present in the church in every age. But in previous eras there have been factors of restraint which have not been present of late in the West. We may suppose it was difficult for the early church to trivialize the gospel because they lived so very close to the time of Christ himself and the apostles. Furthermore, they were often face to face with the stern realities of martyrdom. In such a situation, they had the faith to believe the gospel in its grandeur and mystery, even if they often mis-stated it theologically.

The Middle Ages were a period when miracle, mystery and sin were looked upon as everyday factors of the world in which man lives. The fault in this age was to exaggerate the miraculous and to invest buildings, relics, martyrs and saints with a quality of mystery which was superstitious and unwarrantable. This was their error and their sin. It was a great fault and one from which the modern world may be thankful to have escaped. But there is at least this much to be said for the medieval outlook, that it did not, generally speaking, evaporate away all the mystery of the faith or reduce it to 'the light of common day'.

It is very much to the honour and credit of the Protestant Reformers of the sixteenth century that they exorcized the ghost of superstition from the church of their day without destroying a proper appreciation of the supernatural. The Reformers were first and foremost religious men. That is to say, they were not primarily scholars or technical experts in the letter of Scripture. They were not even primarily academic theologians. They had all of these skills and many more. But they were supremely the men they were because they were men of God and ministers of Christ. Their writings are the evidence of this fact. None more so than Calvin's *Institutes*, which is a book about religion rather than a textbook on theology. The pages of Calvin's writings are instinct with a sense of the ineffable greatness of God and of our consequent obligation to love, serve, obey and enjoy him. Calvin is not content to inform the mind. He challenges the conscience and warms the heart. His motive is to save his hearers, not just to educate them.

A high sense of the mystery of the faith was maintained by the great divines of the seventeenth and eighteenth centuries. But in the last century a change came. Apart from certain more privileged areas—especially those favoured by religious revivals—the tendency in the past hundred years in the West has been for Christians to lose a sense of the mystery of the faith.

The consequence of this has inevitably been that the gospel has been brought down to man's level. Its profundities have not been appreciated. Its sublimities have not been scaled by the modern Christian mind. Its fullness has not been appreciated by our busy age. And therefore our character, as Christians, has reflected less and less of that 'other-worldliness' which was once the hall-mark of the believer and which former generations always expected to find in men professing to be converted.

It is to be feared that a future generation, when it looks back on our age of Christianity, will have to make the dreadful assessment of us that we were an age of shallowness in the things of God. That is not to deny that we have attained to a fair degree of soundness in the letter of doctrinal understanding as evangelical believers. But our age has been sadly deficient in what may be termed spiritual greatness. At the root of this is the modern disease of shallowness. We are all too impatient to meditate on the faith we profess. We cannot say, 'O the depth!'

Modern Christians quickly feel they have 'had enough' when they meet with a more serious attitude towards gospel mysteries than they are used to. But men deceive themselves if they imagine they can flit like a butterfly from one religious excitement to another and consider they have done their duty to God without ever pausing to be amazed at the heights and depths of God's grace. It is not the busy skimming over religious books or the careless hastening through religious duties which makes for a strong Christian faith. Rather, it is unhurried meditation on gospel truths and the exposing of our minds to these truths that yields the fruit of sanctified character.

There are a number of areas where it would be profitable for us as modern Christians to recover more 'depth' in our grasp of the gospel. We may notice the following:

1. *A deeper sense of the sinfulness of sin*

This is one area in which we today have parted company with earlier Evangelicals. Modern Christianity is impatient of anything beyond a perfunctory confession of sin. It is generally felt that a believer is entitled to live for hours and days in the pursuit of secular duties and interests with little pause for private prayer or worship. Many Christians of this class are content to utter a cheery 'Father, forgive me' and go on their way through life. But such a Christianity is too 'healthy' and too confident by half.

11

Ought not a believer regularly to call himself to account for his sins in the presence of God? Ought he not frequently in life to stir himself up to reflect on the odiousness of sin and its guiltiness in God's sight? Shall Christ be brought to a state of death and damnation because of sin, and shall the Christian not remind himself on occasion that *every* sin he commits deserves God's wrath and curse both in this life and in that to come? There is a place in the life of a real Christian for *self-loathing* for our sin [*Ezek.* 36:31]. There is a place for *feeling* our uncleanness as well as confessing it [*Isa.* 6:5]. If our earlier Protestant divines could speak of their sin as 'infinity on infinity' and 'infinity multiplied by infinity', what ought other believers to say of theirs?

It is the besetting sin of our age to trivialize sin. The remedy is to meditate on the holiness and righteousness of God himself, on the strictness and perfection of his laws, on the agonies of the damned in hell and, above all, on the sufferings of our blessed Redeemer on the cross of Calvary. The Christian stops making spiritual progress as soon as he stops repenting. The modern fashion is to skip through a few words of confession as though sin were no more serious to God than the omission of some detail of etiquette or the infringement of table-manners.

Let us recall that sin is the contradiction of God. The best saints have looked into their own hearts as into a bottomless pit of corruption or an ocean of depravity. They were right to do so. It is something we need to learn from them all over again. Of our sins, we might say, 'O the depth!'

2. *A deeper attitude of reverence in worship*

It was said of the early church that its attitude to God was characterized by 'fear' [*Acts* 2:43] and sometimes by 'great fear' [*Acts* 5:5,11]. The apostle Paul instructs the Christians of his day to behave in their congregational worship services in such a way that the outsider may have the secrets of his heart made manifest. The awareness of God's Being was to lead him to fall down on his face confessing, 'God is in you of a truth' [*1 Cor.* 14:25]. The whole tone of apostolic teaching regarding God's service and worship is that it should be 'with reverence and godly fear' [*Heb.* 12:28]. Indeed, our whole salvation is to be worked out with 'fear and trembling' [*Phil.* 2:12]. Fear must never be absent.

However, this 'fear' or reverence has very largely been lost in modern services of worship. It is partly because the spirit of our age is one of superficiality. The modern man rushes in 'where angels fear to tread'. He goes to God confidently and in a flurry of unprepared thoughts, words and emotions. Indeed, the older practice of preparing for worship at God's house by first spending time in secret prayer is generally discounted as an unwelcome and a burdensome addition to the day's religious agenda.

It is greatly to be deplored that many evangelical church services appear to be entirely unmarked by reverence or godly fear. It is a thousand pities that deep seriousness in public worship is a thing of the past almost everywhere. A vast deal of culpable ignorance lies behind the bustle of modern church services. But the deepest fault of all is our lack of appreciation of the glory, greatness and majesty of the God whom we have come to worship.

It ought to be a rule that when we come to God's house we do not talk about our ordinary affairs more than is strictly essential and that even our exchange of greetings be made with a respectful hush. Our whole attention is to be taken up with the duty of the hour, which is to exercise our souls and voices in giving devout praise to the Almighty, and careful audience to his Word.

Our thoughts must be re-educated to have a high view of God, especially when we are in the house of prayer. When we pray to God, we are to put ourselves down low in his presence and bend our minds to the task of concentrating on his infinite greatness. This is the way to have our hearts warmed and cheered, because God 'giveth grace to the humble' [*James* 4:6]. But the careless and the impertinent go away unblessed because they have not 'sanctified him in their hearts' [*1 Pet.* 3:15].

We are to pay heed to what we sing to God and pour out our hearts to him with grace and not in an unthinking torrent of sound, as if God listened only to the voice and not to the music of our hearts. In hearing sermons, we are to give heed to the doctrine and its application to our lives, not allowing ourselves to be distracted by any supposed infirmity in the preacher's voice, style or delivery. If we get little from the sermon, let us augment it by gathering later with Christian friends to discuss the main points. By gathering up the crumbs afterwards we may greatly increase what we received in church. 'Holiness becomes God's house' always [*Ps.* 93:5]. We need to remember that when we come to public worship we are coming to something excellent and heavenly. Of true worship, it might be said, 'O the depth!'

3. *We are to have a high view of God's intention to bless the world*

This is very evidently what the apostle Paul had in mind when he originally penned the words which form the title of this article. The sweep of Paul's mind takes in the entire course of human history. God, he declares, is planning to bless all mankind. In the Old Testament he confined his blessing to Israel. In the present age of the New Testament he is largely confining his blessing to the Gentiles. In a coming day, before the end, Israel is to be spiritually revived. There will be a 'fullness' of salvation for Israel and for the whole world. It is an astounding assertion which Paul makes here when he contemplates the plan of God as it becomes effectual in human history: 'God hath concluded them all in unbelief, that he might have mercy upon all' [*Rom.* 11:32]. This does not, of course, mean that all will be saved but that all believers will be saved. They will come to Christ out of all nations and they will all attribute their deliverance from unbelief to the mere mercy and grace of God.

Out of the depths of sin and guilt is being called a new, redeemed humanity, elect according to divine purpose. No force on earth will stop them from hearing the gospel or from believing it and persevering to the end. They will be called to the foot of the cross in spite of every prejudice of their upbringing and disadvantages of their personal circumstances. Grace will not only make them surrender to the Saviour. It will make them do so gladly, voluntarily, lovingly.

The bigoted devotee to false religion will be brought by grace to bow the knee to Christ and the former materialist will be turned into a heavenly-minded worshipper of the one true God. Every barrier which formerly separated between them will be abolished. No consideration of colour, creed or rank will spoil the unity in Christ which God's redeemed people will enjoy at last. This is the destiny which awaits the true people of God and their righteousness is all of him.

It is no wonder, with such thoughts before him as these, that Paul can cry out, 'O the depth!' Our God is the only God. His purpose alone will succeed and triumph on earth. All his opponents and haters will come to nothing. All who love and serve him will inherit glory and immortality. God has many elect persons still to be called by the gospel. Our labour is not in vain in the Lord. Let courage characterize our witness for Jesus and let us pray for a larger vision of God's purpose. Only in that way will our modern churches rise above the shallow spirit of this age.

3

The Still Small Voice

There is nothing about God's being, nature or ways which embarrasses us more than his gentleness. We readily think of power, majesty, greatness and sovereignty when we remember God. It is right and good that we should do so. These are all parts of his ways. They do not surprise or unman us because we expect them and are, in a manner, prepared for them. But God's gentleness is somehow awesome and overwhelming to our minds. It catches us off balance and staggers us by its very wonderfulness.

No doubt Noah felt such deep emotions of tenderness and awe when, after the flood, he saw the beauty and stillness of the rainbow in the heavens above his head. The old world was gone forever. Sinners and the memory of their sin were now blotted out. The crashing of divine wrath was, on this occasion, over. A vast calm and stillness covered the earth as at the beginning. The bow of God's fury was laid aside, his arrows returned to their quiver. In its place appeared the bow of covenant mercy, certified by the express promise from the lips of God himself that there would never be another universal flood to wipe out the earth. As Noah drank in the sight of this covenant sign in the clouds he doubtless covered his face in grateful worship. The God of power is as terrible in his gentleness as in his vengeance.

There was an occasion when Moses, newly disappointed and angered by the idolatry of his people [*Exod.* 32-34], needed the fresh strength which comes only from sacred communion with God. On the solitary heights of Sinai he bathed his vexed spirit in the calm delight afforded him by the gracious presence of Jehovah. With the boldness born of holy intimacy he cries out to the Lord, 'Show me thy glory' [*Exod.* 33:18]. It is the highest request that any man can ask of God, and it was granted—at least, so far as it was possible for Moses to bear it: 'It shall come to pass, while my glory passeth by, that I will put thee in a cleft of the rock and will cover thee with my hand while I pass by; and I will take away mine hand, and thou shalt see my back parts: but my face shall not be seen' [*Exod.* 33:22-23].

It is not easy to explain all aspects of Moses' experience on that occasion. But he must assuredly have had a keen awareness of the tender care which is so apparent from the narrative. The divine 'hand' which for a time protected and covered him was removed only when it was safely possible for Moses to open his eyes on the uncreated glory of the God who is 'a consuming fire' [*Heb.* 12:29]. Among the emotions which moved him at the experience to 'bow his head and worship' [*Exod.* 34:8] was, we suggest, a loving appreciation that the God of eternal splendours is infinitely gentle in his dealings with those who love him.

The famous experience of Isaiah in the temple [*Isa.* 6] has more of gentleness in it than we commonly notice. We are apt to pay attention to the sublime vision of the Lord lifted up and overawing all created beings, and to the experience of numinous awe, with its accompanying sense of sin, which the prophet underwent. These aspects are certainly present and they are central. But there is more divine pity and kindness than we sometimes pause to appreciate.

What more appropriate acts of love could the Almighty have

given to the alarmed prophet than were given on that occasion? Both by symbolic gesture and by verbal revelation, he was assured that his sin was entirely removed. Further, he received an immediate call to the prophetic ministry in order to save out of his guilty nation those elect persons who would continue the church's testimony till a better day would dawn.

When the soul of man is hot with a burning sense of sinfulness, nothing is so welcome as the immediate removal of guilt and the accompanying assurance that God remembers it no more. And when a man is brought to see the sinfulness of society around him, nothing so quietens his grief as the permission and command of God to preach to men the Word of truth. In both respects the gentleness and grace of God towards Isaiah are marvellously present in the experience.

The gentleness of God, however, comes to expression in one episode of the Old Testament which is exceptionally instructive. We refer to the time when Elijah stood before God on Horeb [1 Kings 19:8-19]. No contrast could be greater than that between the prophet's triumph in the previous chapter and his sense of failure in this. The consequent emotional stress and strain on the great man of God are clear enough from the narrative: 'He requested for himself that he might die' [1 Kings 19:4].

But the prayer for death, as so often with tired preachers, is but the effect of disappointment and a sense of failure. In his exquisite care, Jehovah surrounds him with special providences and experiences which reveal the measure of his preciousness to the God who called him to this difficult ministry. An angel must bake food for him. An angel must minister affectionate advice to him and bid him draw aside from ordinary duty to hold a therapeutic interview with the King of glory himself. It is exceptional treatment by any standard and it proves the nearness of God's care to tired servants in their time of trouble.

There is more, however, in this experience of Elijah on Horeb, and it is to one particular aspect of what took place there that we wish to draw attention—the 'still small voice' [*1 Kings* 19:12]. God displayed before the prophet's eyes a succession of breath-taking and spectacular exhibitions of divine power: a mighty wind, an earthquake and then a fire. Impressive as each dramatic display was, it had in it a deficiency to which the Lord himself repeatedly draws attention. Three times over we are told that 'the LORD was not in' these things.

The lesson to be learnt from this remarkable passage of Scripture is clear. The most sublime of God's works are not his prodigious acts of power but his acts of grace. B. B. Warfield handles the whole passage with consummate skill in one of his printed sermons.[1] But our particular concern now is to stress the wonderful truth in the passage that God's power is seen to best effect more in his gentleness than in his acts of force. What, after all, is the highest expression of God's greatness and glory? It is not his outward displays of vast energy in the material world, wonderful as these are, but his inward acts of grace, performed silently in the hearts and lives of men.

It will repay our time and effort to reflect a little on what the *grace* of God is. It is a term we use frequently but seldom appreciate for what it is. The grace of God is his infinite power used gently and for our eternal good. There is something overwhelming about an infinite, all-powerful Being acting with infinite gentleness. Elijah felt it to be so. 'He wrapped his face in his mantle' [*1 Kings* 19:13]. This he did, not when he heard the rending and convulsion of rocks, but when he heard the 'still small voice' of God. It is too much for our emotions when we discover that the Almighty is infinitely tender and infinitely compassionate. It shames our crude notions of God's power and reminds us that his ways are 'above our ways' as the heaven is above the earth [*Isa.* 55:8].

Perhaps it is one of the besetting sins of fallen human nature that we all put too much store by the dramatic, the sensational and the impressive. It comes out very often in the way we give our testimony, or the value we put on others' testimonies. It comes out, too, in the raw notions we sometimes hear about when men claim to be 'filled with the Spirit'. The feeling which comes naturally to us is that God cannot be doing anything important if it is not done according to the noisy standards which we set for him. It is all too easy for us to equate 'life' with excitement and bustling activity. Similarly, we may fall into this same state of mind when we think about religious revival.

But it is not true to say that noise, sensational occurrence and dramatic activity, whatever part they may at times play in the life of an awakened church, are of the essence of God's activity. On the contrary, the most important acts of God's power are those which, all unnoticed by man, touch the secret springs of his soul and heart. Regeneration, sanctification, repentance, growth in grace—all are the product of divine omnipotence acting with marvellous gentleness and love upon man's inner being. These do certainly issue at times in violent praying, striving and crying. But the most vital and central aspect is not that which results in much noise but in much delight in God for his own sake.

No expression of divine omnipotence and grace comes near to that which is to be seen in the incarnation, life and saving actions of the Lord Jesus Christ. Yet here again there is a noticeable muting by God of all sensationalism. The coming of God into our flesh, an event which might well have been trumpeted by every angel from the balconies of glory above, passed almost unnoticed except by a few select persons like Anna, Simeon, some shepherds and a few wise men. No event in history was greater. Scarcely any passed off so unmarked by what we might call the spectacular. There were angels certainly, but their exultant cries were heard by only a select few.

The life of Christ, and his ministry especially, was full of the miraculous and the supernatural. But even here we see a divine restraint. 'He shall not strive, nor cry; neither shall any man hear his voice in the streets' [*Matt.* 12:19]. Nowhere in the ministry of our Lord do we see the slightest hint of divine power exhibited ostentatiously. Men, even the best, act occasionally in bad taste, but God never. Power is never used meaninglessly by God. All is wise, controlled and for a moral purpose.

Grace, we have argued, is God's infinite power working gently in order to bring us to himself. We do not mean by 'gently' that it is not equally infinite with other exercises of power, such as the creation of the world. But we draw attention to the fact that the effect upon the recipient is always benign and welcome. God saves no man to his harm. And God saves none against his will. Grace makes the sinner willing. It is a secret exercise of omnipotence on the hidden man of the heart coaxing and alluring him to salvation and glory by Christ. It is always effectual but it is never brute strength.

There is much for us to learn from this aspect of God's power. Perhaps we are too frequently guilty of limiting God to methods of blessing us which are according to our own understanding. Doubtless our age attaches far too much importance to visible and even spectacular happenings in the life of the church. God, after all, is always working his gracious purpose out on earth, whether seen by us or unseen. Is our faith so weak that we must always have external signs of God's activity, according to our puny expectations? Unceasing, yet unhasting, the God of destiny is moving all things to their foreseen goal. 'Not by might nor by power' are all things to be brought to pass but by the Spirit who works as he will.

4

Ceasing From Man

'Cease ye from man, whose breath is in his nostrils: for
wherein is he to be accounted of?' [*Isa.* 2:22]. These
notable words of Isaiah come at the end of a sublime
passage about 'the day of the Lord', a day when all human pride
of achievement would be laid low in the dust and God alone
would be glorified. Nothing would be spared in that day. Trees,
hills, towers, fenced walls, ships and pictures would be thrown
down by the jealousy and righteous anger of God, when he
would arise 'to shake terribly the earth'. Amid the ruins of this
general collapse would be found, strewn on the ground, the idols
and images of sinful men who, in their terror, would cast them
out of sight to the moles and bats, blind creatures like their
very gods. All the pride of mankind is depicted as laid low. Proud
sinners themselves are portrayed as fleeing into the clefts of
the rocks to escape from the avenging wrath of God, who is displeased at the haughtiness and insolent arrogance of men.

Whatever reference such awesome words may have to events
in past history, they have about them an ominous ring which
powerfully suggests that their highest fulfilment will only be in
the last great day of judgement. Here then we are presented with
a spectacle of the overthrow to be made by a righteous God of
all things and all persons who have in any way provoked the eyes

of God's holiness in the course of mankind's history. Civilizations will in a moment be swept away, the monuments and memorials of human self-aggrandizement and all the rotten rags of humanity's corrupt religions will be torn down, stamped in the dust and put to an everlasting disgrace.

There is no mistaking the central purpose of all this earth-shattering divine destruction. It is in order to challenge the false place which sinful man has arrogated to himself in the created order. Once and again we are informed that 'the Lord alone shall be exalted in that day' [*Isa.* 2:11,17] and that every created eye will be impressed (O welcome change!) with the glory of *God's* 'majesty' [19,21]. It is for this reason, so the elevated prophecy informs us, that the Lord at that time will arise 'to shake terribly the earth' [19,21].

Unregenerate man, so long the usurper of the centre-stage position in affairs, is to be put wholly off the stage in the great day of the Lord. All the wretched expressions of man's abominable pride and idolatry are, at last and eternally, to be toppled and brought to extinction. Man in that day will feel himself to be the nothing he is. God will be all in all.

The picture set before us in this passage of the Word of God is full of sobering lessons. It reminds us, for one thing, that the world goes on from day to day only because of the long-suffering and amazing patience of God. All pride, all human haughtiness, all boasting in man's achievement is a fearful forgetting of God Almighty and a dangerous provocation of his holy Name. Then, too, it shows us how ominously suggestive are the temporal judgements of God which are daily occurring before our eyes in this life.

Here a nation falls victim to drought, there to a war, somewhere else to economic collapse, in a fourth place to mortal disease. What are all these temporal changes in the world but so

23

many reminders to the children of God that the Lord is daily shaking terribly the earth because of the pride and idolatry of men and nations? These things are so many finger-posts to men of faith to keep us in mind of the great fact that God will at last shake 'not the earth only, but also heaven' [*Heb.* 12:26]. In that day only one kingdom will remain standing, and only one Man will lift up his head on high amidst the remnants of mankind's shattered glory, our Lord Jesus Christ, whose right alone it is to rule and to reign for ever.

The words of Isaiah 2:22 form the concluding advice given by God to us in the light of the carnage and terminal devastation to come at last upon all the earth. It is similar in many ways to the counsel given by Peter to believers at the close of his second epistle: 'Seeing that all these things shall be dissolved [destroyed], what manner of persons ought ye to be in all holy conversation and godliness?' [*2 Pet.* 3:11].

It is as though the voice of God were heard floating over the wreck of ages on the great day with its solemn echo reverberating back in time to us who live before the event: 'See, this is to be the end of all man's temporary greatness and glory. Therefore be wise and make no more of man than is his proper due. Man is but dust and all his glory will shortly descend into the grave with him. Therefore take your eyes off man, whose breath is in his nostrils. What, after all, is he in the scale of eternal values? Of sinful, proud man, make nothing. Of God your Maker and Judge make more and more. Make God, indeed, your everything. Glory in God alone as you would wish to do when the great day dawns of which I have given you this verbal picture. Glorify God only.'

It is certain that our interpretation of Isaiah's vision here is fully in accordance with other, similar passages of the Word of God. The coming of the great day of the Lord is depicted by

Christ in these terms: 'Then shall all the tribes of the earth mourn, and they shall see the Son of man coming in the clouds of heaven with power and great glory' [*Matt.* 24:30].

Paul refers to the same event in these words: 'When they shall say, Peace and safety; then sudden destruction cometh upon them, as travail upon a woman with child; and they shall not escape' [*1 Thess.* 5:3].

John, in the Book of Revelation, places the same momentous event before our eyes in the following graphic language: 'And the kings of the earth, and the great men, and the rich men, and the chief captains, and the mighty men, and every bondman, and every free man, hid themselves in the dens and in the rocks of the mountains and said to the mountains and rocks, Fall on us, and hide us from the face of him that sitteth on the throne, and from the wrath of the Lamb: For the great day of his wrath is come; and who shall be able to stand?' [*Rev.* 6:15-17] .

The aspect of the great day to which we draw attention in these inspired portraits is that *man* is to be humbled and brought low for his sinful pride. What lies at the very heart of all sin is self-flattery, that good opinion of ourselves which loves to be praised by our fellow-creatures. That it is obnoxious to God is obvious from the fierceness of his anger displayed in his finally uprooting all man's pride and prostrating it by a total overthrow. The three early judgements of God at the Flood, the Tower of Babel and on Sodom teach exactly the same lesson. Human pride kindles a jealousy in God which must 'burn to lowest hell' if man will not repent and humble himself in time.

A DIFFICULT LESSON TO LEARN

It is difficult to learn this lesson that we are to 'cease from man'. Man since the Fall has become so much 'the rubbish of an Adam' that he is constantly robbing God of glory and ascribing to himself an importance which is not rightfully his.

Every sphere in which we live has become a theatre of praise for man. Politics, sport, the arts, science—often even religion too—are usually organized in a manner which throws far too bright a light on the achievements of men. Their names are elevated into headlines, passed in awe from mouth to mouth, surrounded with a halo of false glory and set up as great models to watch and even to follow. The world wonders with great admiration as their human idols pass before their gaze. It is the spirit of this world and, probably to an excessive degree, the spirit of our own age.

The tragedy is that this spirit too quickly becomes the spirit of Christian people also. When that begins to be the case there are always ministers and leaders who are glad to have it so, and who will oblige the willing audience by acting the part of a religious puppet. Where this happens, congregations come to church to be stroked and caressed with soft words which tickle their fancy, and not to be made afraid in the sight of a holy God for their sin and levity.

The gospel minister should be heard, and not seen. He is 'a voice crying in the wilderness'. He is there to proclaim a message on behalf of his Master. He is not in the pulpit in order to ingratiate himself with the people at the expense of the truth which he proclaims. His voice, delivery, dress and bearing ought all to be consistent with the gravity of his message, which must be to humble man and elevate God in sinners' eyes.

If the preacher's motto is 'Woe is me if I preach not the gospel' (as it was Paul's), the people's motto should be: 'Cease ye from man, whose breath is in his nostrils'. That is to say, congregations must discipline and reform themselves to pay attention to the preacher's message and not to the man who delivers it. There is too much reason to fear that there are gospel ministers today who are grasping for men's praises and are not content with the praise and honour which come from God only. And there is too much evidence to suggest that many of those in the pew are forgetting that Paul and Apollos and Cephas are nothing, but only 'stewards of the mysteries of God' [*1 Cor.* 4:1].

A TEST OF ALL OUR RELIGION

The words 'Cease ye from man, whose breath is in his nostrils' are a test of all that we do in the name of Christ. The way in which we conduct our religious services and meetings ought to result in men's going home chastened and impressed with a sense of the glory of God and his greatness. Awe, amazement and fear are the proper reactions to attending a service of worship. There will be times when we wish to go away from the church in silence and to speak to no one but God. There will be times when we desire to conceal our tears and our sighs from our fellow-creatures after hearing the Word preached. There will doubtless too be times when we are exhilarated, inspired, energized and excited. But such spiritual moods will not altogether lack a holy fear and reverence also.

It follows from the principles of religion implied by the words 'Cease ye from man' that there ought never to be entertainment in God's house as a part of divine worship. Entertainment may have its place occasionally. But its place is never in the worship of God. This is not to deny Luther's point that real preaching is in the highest sense entertainment. What we contend for is that the house of God is for other uses than merriment.

Those are the best services and that is the best singing where God is treated with most respect. He is the best preacher who most often impresses those present with the realities of another world. They are the poorest preachers who treat God's house as a place of laughter and amusement and who attach their hearers to themselves by spoon-feeding them what they know the people want rather than by nourishing them with what they need. There will come a time when the serious Christian will have to vote with his feet if he finds he has a minister who acts the clown in the house of the Lord.

The believer must also learn something else from the text which forms the focus of our study. There is a habit of mind required of us by God which may be called self-abasement. This ought to be our daily pursuit. In the light of God's majesty and glory, it becomes us to take a low place and to entertain mean thoughts of ourselves. That commentator is surely correct who states that the term 'pride of life' [1 John 2:16] implies that pride will be our life-long vice. It is found to be so by every exercised believer. There is no instrument in this life able to cut the root of pride wholly out of man's heart.

The way of self-mortification is irksome to flesh and blood but it is the only safe way. Pride follows our heels more closely than our very shadow. It cannot be beaten away or bribed away. It is a cancer of the soul. It acts like acid upon our graces. It swells us up with ludicrous self-importance. It chokes the life of prayer, stifles our usefulness, and will, if not brutally treated, sap the spiritual life within us almost to death.

How relevant these words of Isaiah are to us in our generation: 'Cease ye from man, whose breath is in his nostrils'! It is advice and admonition which ought to be held up on banners everywhere. It is a text which might serve as a perfect antidote to the spirit of our age. While we make so much of man we put off the day of blessing. With one breath we pray for revival and with the next we grieve away God's gracious Spirit by our carnal adulation. We pray for powerful preachers to be raised up and then we ruin them by our flattery. We ask God for good sermons but see too much in the men who preach them to us and take too little thought for God in what is preached.

If we overdo our praise of men we shall provoke God to take them away. Or else we shall provoke him to expose us to the feet of clay which our idols have. 'My glory will I not give to another' [*Isa.* 42:8], says the Almighty and what he says he means with reference to persons secular and also spiritual.

A NECESSARY QUALIFICATION

There is a way of straining and misusing the necessity of ceasing from man which it is no part of our purpose to encourage. The proper way to keep a minister humble is not to discourage, undervalue or be awkward to him. Sad to say, there are misguided persons in some congregations who regard it as their special calling in life to 'keep the preacher humble'. By this they mean that they see it their duty to be a constant thorn in his side. Such persons are nothing but a scourge and a menace.

The proper way in which to ensure the humility of a faithful preacher of the Word of God is to be a model of spirituality. We may and must love our faithful ministers. But we look beyond them to the uncreated God who is their Master and Judge. We attribute infallibility only to the Lord himself. As for men, we are glad when they are gifted and able. But we call to mind that the church's most gifted men have sometimes been her greatest enemies, and her ablest scholars have occasionally done her the greatest harm.

Remembering these things, and calling to mind the nearness of the great day of the Lord we might well decide to 'cease from man, whose breath is in his nostrils'.

29

5

The Interpretation of Providence in History

The occurrence of the word 'interpretation' in the title of this chapter informs us at once that we are in the realm of applied, rather than theoretical or abstract theology. All sciences have their theoretical and their applied aspects. This is true of theology, which, in better days, was regarded as the 'queen of the sciences'. What follows, therefore, is not so much a statement as an argument, or a case. It is an attempt to develop an interpretation of God's providence in history which is true to the Scriptures and practically relevant to the pastoral needs of God's people in the times through which we are now passing.

The general theme of providence is that of God's sovereign and perfect control of all events. There is a natural division of the subject into two aspects: the providence of God in the lives of individuals, and God's providence over nations and over civilization as a whole. Perhaps it would be convenient to give descriptive terms to these two distinct, though related, ways of studying God's providence. We could speak of micro-providence as that which concerns the individual, and macro-providence as that which relates to the larger units of mankind in history. It is with the latter that we are concerned here, and especially with the Christian church in the Anglo-Saxon world.

It needs to be said that the literature which deals with this subject is at one and the same time vast and yet sparse. Whilst all works of history and biography have some tangential connection with the theme, yet books which deal directly and specifically with this subject are, to our knowledge, few in number. That is not altogether surprising because the exercise of interpreting providence is essentially a religious and spiritual, rather than a purely historical, one. It is a task which we can only begin with any degree of realism once we have accepted the great (and nowadays highly unpopular) postulate that God is truly known only in the Christian Scriptures and that history has ethical and spiritual meaning because it is the unfolding of a divine purpose.

Such a great spiritual classic as Flavel's *The Mystery of Providence*, therefore, will not help us greatly, because it deals with the more individual aspect of this theme. Indeed, most treatments of providence naturally tend to look at it from the point of view of the individual, especially that of the Christian believer. This is not true of a recent valuable study entitled *The Providence of God* by Benjamin Wirt Farley,[1] a contemporary American scholar. Professor Farley's book provides us with a very thorough historical survey of providence. That is to say, he works his way comprehensively, first through the views of providence held by the great thinkers of Greece and Rome, then by the early Church Fathers, and then by the Schoolmen, the Reformers and so on, up to the present day. It is a book to which one will turn again and again for information about the opinions of writers through the ages. But it does not set out to address itself directly to the type of application of the theme which forms the title of this chapter. Rather than beginning with the books, therefore, it will be better to take our point of departure from the Word of God itself.

In Matthew 24 we have the great discourse of the Lord Jesus Christ on the subject of the Last Things. There our Lord is informing his people of the most notable and significant events which would occur in the course of human history right up to the very end. More particularly, Christ predicts the fall of Jerusalem, which occurred in A.D. 70, and also the destruction of the whole world at the Second Coming. From our standpoint today, one event is in the past and the other in the future. And with regard to both these momentous events, Christ says that we are to 'watch' [*Matt.* 24:42]. Clearly, the implication is that Christians are to be awake to major events in this world and they are to attempt to understand them, at least to some extent.

Failure to 'watch' and to be awake to what God is doing in the course of history is, according to Christ's warning, both foolish and dangerous. This is supremely true of the unbelieving world. But it is also true of God's own people. If we do not 'watch', then we are likely to become either complacent or, alternatively, discouraged. Events in the external world are integrally related to the words of Holy Scripture. To be ignorant of Scripture is to be unprepared for what God is doing in history. To be unprepared at the end, when Christ returns, is to lose our soul eternally.

Furthermore, the view we take of events between our own day and the end of the world will inevitably have a considerable effect upon our whole state of mind as Christians. If we look for nothing in the future but gloom and declension, then we shall be pessimistic as to the degree of success which preaching and missionary endeavour will have on earth. But if we have an optimistic eschatology, we shall be correspondingly affected in our outlook and in our expectation of coming blessing. This is particularly true of the way in which we interpret the passage in Romans 11 respecting the 'mystery' of Israel. Admittedly, it may amount to no more than our state of mind as we set to work in the task of proclaiming the gospel and praying for its success. But our morale is very important. The overall view of providence which we adopt will have a close bearing on our morale and our degree of expectation in God's work.

SOME BIBLICAL INSIGHTS

The passage from 1 Kings 18:17-18 is of considerable significance for the subject in hand. It consists of a snatch of conversation between the great prophet Elijah and the infamous King Ahab. There had been a serious state of drought in the kingdom for three and a half years. Each man, interestingly enough, blamed the other for the troubles, evidently for exactly opposite reasons:

> And it came to pass, when Ahab saw Elijah, that Ahab said
> unto him, Art thou he that troubleth Israel? And he answered,
> I have not troubled Israel; but thou, and thy father's house, in
> that ye have forsaken the commandments of the Lord, and
> thou hast followed Baalim.

Ahab's point of view was that Elijah had interrupted the peace and happiness of the land by praying down God's judgement. Elijah's opinion of the matter was that Ahab's idolatry had been the real cause of ruin to the land. It is an instructive exchange between a man of God and a man of the world. To the worldly man, it is the 'sour churchman' who spoils life. To the man of God, it is the reckless sinner who ruins the world by bringing God's curse upon a land. In Ahab's opinion, Israel was *his* kingdom and Elijah was a nuisance. In Elijah's judgement, Israel was *God's* kingdom and Ahab was a thorn in its flesh. It is a notable case of two opposing interpretations of providence.

33

There is a point of major importance to be noticed in this exchange between Ahab and Elijah. *A man's theology always determines his view of providence.* It must be so and it cannot be otherwise. What we think of God must determine our interpretation of what we see all around us, both in the church and in the world. This principle is to be found everywhere in the Bible. If we apply the principle to our modern situation, especially in Britain, we shall see that the principle is both a true and a useful one. Who, it might be asked, are the 'troublers of Israel' in Britain today? Every man answers instinctively in terms of his own theology. The Ecumenical finds the 'troublers of Israel' in those who will not lay aside every doctrinal difference and 'heal the wounds in the body of Christ'. The Charismatic in turn blames the church's troubles on those who decline to seek the 'gifts'. The theological Liberal traces the modern church's malady to the presence still on earth of an 'antediluvian confessionalism'. The Evangelical and the Calvinist diagnose the church's ills as the judgement of God upon theological unfaithfulness and departure from Scripture.

This principle holds good also in its reverse form. *The way a man interprets providence proves his real theology.* This is illustrated interestingly by a recently published book, entitled *Defending and Declaring the Faith.*[2] From the title, one would expect to find that the orthodox creed of evangelical religion was being set forth and defended. The author looks at the life and thought of eight well known Scottish theologians and preachers between 1860 and 1920. It is valuable as a summary of the thought of such men as Kennedy of Dingwall, John Caird, A. B. Bruce and James Denney. But what is surprising to the evangelical reader is a comparison between the title of the book and the foreword. The author of the foreword admires and praises John McLeod Campbell, Thomas Erskine of Linlathen, and Edward Irving.

Yet all three of these men, far from defending the faith, were men of unsound views. They were disciplined for unorthodoxy by the nineteenth-century Scottish church to which they belonged! So here is a remarkable instance of an hiatus between the title of a book and its message. What today is being called the church's remedy was, in better days, treated as heresy.

This brings us to a further point in the church's duty in a time of judgement and declension to enquire after the real cause of the trouble. A generation which makes a false diagnosis of the church's ills may land the church in apostasy. There are repeated warnings in the prophets against the folly of either not heeding, or else misinterpreting, the omens of providence [Cf. *Isa.* 22:12-14, *Jer.* 23:16-17, *Ezek.* 22:28-30]. This is what Ezekiel caustically terms 'daubing the wall with untempered mortar' [*Ezek.* 22:28], which is later defined as 'seeing false burdens and causes of banishment' [*Lam.* 2:14]. In the New Testament, Christ refers to this same sin as a culpable failure to 'discern the signs of the times' [*Matt.* 16:3].

Whatever be the true causes of the church's steep decline in Britain in our generation, there is no denying that the decline is there. There is a worm at the root of the tree which threatens not the leaf or the blossom only, but the very existence of the tree itself. Britain has no patent rights to the gospel of Christ. The church of Christ as such cannot be lost. But national churches can be lost. The Jewish church in Palestine was lost for hundreds of years after A.D. 70. Much the same happened to North Africa and Turkey at later periods in history. We had better diagnose the cause of our modern ills correctly. Failure to do so might plunge our nation into darkness for centuries. If we see the cause, there is hope that we may repent in time. But who will repent of unrecognized sin? The fearful possibility is that we may already be past hope, because God has given our church leaders over to a reprobate mind. God forbid that it should be so. But the situation is urgent. And it is made all the more urgent in that key concepts of God's providence are out of favour.

SOME 'LOST' CONCEPTS

In the modern church, there are a number of concepts relating to providence which are in danger of being lost for one reason or another. They are concepts which are to be found in, or else to be derived from, the Word of God. They were highly cherished in better ages of the church. Their loss in the modern church has made us spiritually weaker and less able to wrestle with God for a return of his favour. We may look briefly at four such lost concepts.

1. *The concept of a 'model age'.* Not in an absolute sense, certainly, but in a limited sense, there are 'model ages' of the church. By that we mean that, in some ages, God is powerfully and wonderfully at work on earth in sending revival, reformation and influential preachers of the gospel. At other ages there is a dryness and a deadness, even on good and orthodox men. It is true, of course, that the teaching on the church in apostolic times is the only 'model' church in an absolute sense. There we have the inspired men and the blueprint of what the gospel and the church ought to be. But if we see all subsequent church history as nothing more than monotonous shades of grey, we have a false idea of church history. The fact is that some ages have been rich in spiritual greatness while others have been lifeless and dead. There have been recent influences which have led to a disparaging attitude towards such golden ages of the church as the Reformation, the Covenanting and Puritan era and the period of the Evangelical Awakening. But such great ages do come. If we do not believe in them, how can we begin to pray

for such an age to dawn on our country again?

2. *The idea that God must be glorified on earth.* That God is to be glorified is a belief common to all Christians. But that God is to be glorified on earth, by our obedience and faithfulness, is by no means the common creed of all believers as it should be. The point is well illustrated in an anecdote which has come down to us from Scottish Covenanting times. A conforming Christian put the question to a Covenanter as to why he was prepared to suffer such 'unnecessary' trials. 'Because', as he put it, 'I shall have heaven as a Christian and you will get no more.' To this the godly non-conformist replied, 'Yes, we shall have more. We shall have God glorified *on earth*.' There is both great theology and also great heroism in these words.

The practical outworking of the point is that carelessness in our walk, worship and witness not only forfeits God's blessing but robs him of his declarative glory on earth—an incalculable loss. Universal obedience to God's written Word becomes, in the light of this, more essential than life itself. It is an aspect of the truth which needs to be recovered.

3. It belongs to the biblical portrait of God's church on earth that *its history is like a wave, periodically rising and falling.* This is the view of providence implicit in such passages, for instance, as Psalms 44, 78, 106 and 126. Christ himself made it clear that this pattern would continue to the end of the world. There would be times in history 'when the bridegroom' would be 'taken away' from God's people, so that believers would 'fast in those days' [*Mark* 2:20]. Again, the Lord speaks of times in the history of the New Testament church when believers would desire to see 'one of the days of the Son of man, and should not see it' [*Luke* 17:22]. Periods of revival and declension, to use modern terms,

will alternate in the life of Christ's church till the very end.

It is of great importance to believers to be thoroughly convinced of this aspect of God's providence. It kindles afresh our flagging hopes to realize that, however low the cause of Christ may fall, God is able to revive it again, even in a very short time, in answer to believing prayer. The wave that falls to its trough is destined to rise up again to another peak. This concept is essential to us if we are not to sink into despair in such a day as this.

4.   The fourth aspect of God's providence which is in danger of being lost is *the distinctive concept of the church's history which emerged at the Protestant Reformation.* According to this view, there are three clearly defined periods of the church's history: the early period, the medieval period and the modern period. This three-fold view of church history is a more important part of our Protestant heritage than might at first appear. It serves to remind us that for a thousand years the church in the West wandered into darkness and superstition. This is not to deny that there were good and great men in the Middle Ages. But it helps us to see the immense debt of gratitude we owe to God for the Reformers and their work. We must never allow this view of history to be blurred in our minds. The Reformers not only gave us a new principle of exegesis and a new systematic theology but also a new way of looking at church history. This view of history is to be found implicitly in the three Reformation treatises of Luther written in 1520. It is also found more explicitly in the Fourth Book of Calvin's *Institutes* and in Foxe's *Book of Martyrs,* as it is popularly called.

There are today powerful influences at work tending to obscure this attitude to church history, which was once the commonplace view of Protestants. The Oxford Movement of the 1830s seriously challenged this view of providence. But, more recently, it has been blurred in people's minds by the misguided statements of some Protestant leaders, who are suggesting that the Reformation was something of a tragedy or an unfortunate mistake.

If the Reformation comes to be looked on as a tragedy, then Protestants will have ceased to be the real spiritual heirs of the Reformers. To give ground on this point of history is, in effect, to concede to a new theology. There are many who do not appear to see that this is the case. But it must be so. To recover out of the present state of decline, therefore, means that Protestants must go back to the older view of history which looked at the Reformation as a return from darkness to light. *Post tenebras lux* [After darkness, light] is more than a slogan. It is an interpretation of providence. Indeed, it implies a vital creed.

PROVIDENCE AND HISTORY

From what we have said, it follows that the way we interpret providence will determine the way we evaluate history, especially church history. And that, in turn, will determine the way we look at the great figures of church history and those who write about them.

It needs briefly to be said that providence and history are the same thing looked at from two different points of view. Both terms refer to the contents of God's eternal purpose or decree as that unfolds in this world. 'History' is the term we use to refer to the events of God's plan on earth when looked at from the standpoint of mankind. 'Providence' is the term we use when we are looking at the same thing from a theological point of view. Of course, many do not choose to accept that there is such a thing as providence. But that does not concern us here. Christians, at any rate, are committed to a belief in providence, which is just history as God has ordained it and watches over it.

It is important to remember that a man cannot really understand history if he has no true concept of God's providence. It is true that he may be an expert in some of the details and therefore may be worthy of great respect for his erudition. But to be an authority in the details is not the same as to be competent to understand the overall significance of a period of history. An expert may, strange to say, 'miss the wood for the trees'.

One of the most remarkable examples of this is to be seen in Gibbon's *Decline and Fall of the Roman Empire*, which is justly regarded as an historical masterpiece. But as an overall explanation of the subject with which it deals it is unsatisfactory. Gibbon attributes the fall of Rome to its abandonment of paganism and its conversion to Christianity! He was simply reiterating an old pagan view, advanced by such ancient enemies of the gospel as Celsus. Augustine long ago answered their case conclusively in the twenty-two books of his polemical work, *The City of God*. The pagan view had virtually disappeared till Gibbon revived it in late eighteenth-century England. It is a classic case of a timeless work of history marred by a false view of providence. In that case, there was no very great damage done to Christian faith. But in other cases, great damage can be done to men's faith.

Religious and philosophical assumptions always lie at the heart of the way men write history. This point is brought out very clearly in a helpful book by Dr David Bebbington of Stirling University, entitled *Patterns in History*.[3] He shows that history has been viewed from various standpoints over the centuries. He mentions several of these views: the *cyclical* outlook of oriental writers; the traditional Christian view, which considers history to be a *straight line;* the idea of *progress*; the theory of *historicism*, and that of *Marxism*. Perhaps we today would need to include a further view—that of historical relativism. But the essential point made by Dr Bebbington is that there are not only the 'brute facts' of history; there is also the deeper question of how we under-stand and interpret those facts. If those who write about history do not have a biblical view of providence, they will scarcely be able to see the events they write about in their true light.

It is very interesting to evangelical Christians to note that historians who may not share their view of divine providence are nonetheless concerned about the interpretation of history. Sir Arnold Toynbee, for instance, in his monumental work *A Study of History*, speaks about 'metahistory'. He is evidently quot-ing from the historian, Christopher Dawson, who had earlier used the word, on an analogy with the familiar term 'metaphys-ics'. Toynbee explains the word in this way:

> Metahistory is concerned with the nature of history, the mean-
> ing of history and the cause and significance of historical
> change. It arises out of the study of history, and is akin to meta-
> physics and theology. The metahistorian seeks to integrate his
> study of reality in some higher dimension than that of human
> affairs as these present themselves to him phenomenally.[4]

At first sight it may not seem a very important matter how one interprets the events of the past or even of the present. But no one who takes the Christian faith seriously could adopt such an attitude of indifference to the providence of God and its meaning. It is the duty of the church to explain history. The Lord Jesus Christ laid it as a sin upon the Jewish leaders that they had failed to discern the voice of providence in their day: 'O ye hypocrites, ye can discern the face of the sky; but can ye not dis-cern the signs of the times?' [*Matt.* 16:3].

Events, especially events in which the hand of God is mani-fest, have a meaning which we ignore only to our loss or at our peril. Admittedly, there are vast areas of providence which we are not qualified to interpret. But that does not excuse men for their failure to interpret crucial periods of history, such as the life of Christ and the early church, correctly.

The question might well be asked, do we have a key in the Bible by which to interpret events in our day? We believe that we do. The great 'benchmark', so to speak, of modern church history is to be found in the Acts of the Apostles and its inspired account of what God did on and after the Day of Pentecost. In that narrative, along with the other apostolic writings of the New Testament, we have a golden key to the meaning of all subsequent events in the history of the church and, to some extent, even of the world. The New Testament writings show us what real Christianity is, what the church should be, and therefore what we may confidently expect God to bless and to favour on earth.

Consequently, where, in history, we find that same doctrine taught and those same church ordinances practised, there we may be certain that we see the approval of God in his providence. Conversely, where, in history, we see serious departure from New Testament doctrine and practice, there we know we see God's wrath and curse. It seems impossible to escape from this view of the matter, if we grant the premise that the Scriptures are the inerrant Word of God.

The application of the principle here stated drives us towards the conviction that the religion of the Middle Ages was a grave departure from God and that the Reformation was a glorious returning to God. So much is surely clear, whatever else in providence may not be clear. But to be convinced of that is essential and it is enough. It is enough to glorify God by and enough to be saved by, if we are brought in this way to believe in the Christ of the New Testament and of the Reformation.

It is precisely this interpretation of history, however, which is under attack in the western world in the twentieth century. The classic Protestant historians, whose names were once a household word in Christian circles, are now sometimes referred to, even by Evangelicals, as biased and untrustworthy writers. This is the new Protestant judgement upon historians such as Knox, Calderwood, Wodrow and McCrie for Scotland, and Foxe, Burnet, D'Aubigné and Wylie, who chronicled the events of the Protestant Reformation in England and on the continent of Europe.

The argument has now gained ground that a writer like John Knox, in his book *The History of the Reformation in Scotland*, is guilty of prejudice. He identifies his own cause with the cause of God. What favours his cause is praised by him as the work of God and what hinders his cause is reported as the work of God's enemies. That, according to modern writers, is not good history. It is said to be too subjective a view of God's cause and it is thought to vitiate the canons of objectivity required in a reliable writer of history.

The objection sounds plausible enough. But it seems to leave the most crucial factor of all out of the reckoning. It fails to do justice to the New Testament Scriptures. If that religion which the New Testament presents as the truth happens also to be the religion of Knox, then it is justifiable to identify it as the work of God, and its opponents as the enemies of God. The only way to invalidate this conclusion, surely, is to demonstrate that Knox's message and the message of the New Testament were not substantially the same. Knox believed that they were the same. Hence the explanation for his confidence.

The real reason why some modern Protestants apologize for Knox's manner of writing history is that they are no longer in sympathy with the theology which he held. It looks very much like being 'ashamed of the gospel' [*Rom.* 1:16], albeit in a sophisticated way. There is a corollary to the claim made by early Protestants that the Reformation was a glorious work of God's providence. It is this: that God's blessing must be expected to rest on nations embracing the Reformation teachings and his displeasure to follow nations which turn from those teachings.

Whatever view one holds of the rights and wrongs of British rule (and both were there) in the days when this country was in its prime, it cannot be denied that the collapse of our national power went hand in hand with the collapse of our Protestant religion. Sir Arnold Toynbee, to whom we have referred, tells us that he lived to witness both the high water-mark of British power in 1897 and its decline by the year 1972, just seventy-five years later.[5] The dates are significant in that they correspond closely with the decline of the British pulpit. This fact surely illustrates the proverb: 'Righteousness exalteth a nation: but sin is a reproach to any people' [*Prov.* 14:34]. The curse has not come without a cause. Do we need to look any further afield for our metahistory of the period in which we live?

OUR BACKSLIDDEN PROTESTANTISM

Generally speaking, it would appear to be true to say that the backsliding of Britain (and probably of America and some other Anglo-Saxon countries belonging to the Protestant family) has taken place in two stages. As a nation, we rejected the theology of the Reformation about the time of the First World War, and the morality of the Reformation at, or just after, the Second World War. The New Morality and the 'permissive society' appeared in the early 1960s at about the same time. Since then, there has been a marked shift downwards in this country. That is not to deny that there has been, more recently, a recovery of the Reformed faith. But the impact of this movement, intensely promising as it is, is as yet only very small. The point we make here is that society as a whole, and the church as a whole, has sunk steadily further from righteousness and from God. And, until God sends upon us the blessing of true revival, we can only continue to sink still further.

Of the many contributory causes to this state of national decline, we may here mention just three. We believe one to be the secularization of our national school system after the passing of the Education Acts of 1870 (England and Wales) and 1872 (Scotland). After the implementation of these Acts, our day schools, many of which had before been in the hands of the churches and had taught the Protestant catechisms as well as the Bible, steadily moved towards a position of religious 'neutrality'. After the two World Wars, the pace of secularization became accelerated. This has meant not simply that religious education in the traditional sense is now only haphazardly taught, but also that the content of the history syllabus has become chronically anaemic in its treatment of the great spiritual conflict which raged in the sixteenth and seventeenth centuries. But this is the crucially important era.

So much do some far-sighted educators today resent this New History, as it is called, that a society or movement has been started with the name 'The Campaign for Real Education'! No doubt they are dissatisfied with the modern approach to teaching other subjects too. But the new approach to teaching history is singled out in their very first pamphlet as desperately in need of improvement and modification. 'The pursuit of truth has been replaced by what is called "the form of knowledge approach", which means in practice that pupils are encouraged to arrive at confident judgements . . . while being dismissive of "facts" . . . That, like so much else in the New History, is wilfully perverse.'[6] So writes the author of this pamphlet on behalf of this new society, which has the support of MPs, members of the House of Lords and other academics.

A second more powerful and harmful influence upon our

land has come from eminent literary men and women, especially in the period since the First World War. Today we have almost come to accept that eminent literary persons must be irreligious. There are, of course, notable exceptions, such as C. S. Lewis. But this appears to have been the main direction taken by men and women of letters in the past sixty years.

A notable assault on Christian standards of behaviour was made about the time of the First War by the Bloomsbury Group. This was a brilliant set of young Cambridge graduates, including Lytton Strachey, Virginia Woolf, John Maynard Keynes, Duncan Grant and Bertrand Russell. They were later followed by D. H. Lawrence and others. These all had a profound influence on the United Kingdom. The private morality of many of them was a shameless denial of earlier British standards of behaviour and morality. To read Michael Holroyd's biography of Strachey is to see how advanced practical ungodliness had become at that comparatively early date among some of our influential English intellectuals. It was a significant turning-point in the ethical history of this land in modern times. What we see today is not much more than the widespread adoption of their ideals and practices by persons of all sorts. But the lead was taken by these influential figures those many years ago.

The third factor which we may mention as a contributory cause of the present low ebb in our country is the rise of Roman Catholicism to a position of importance and influence unparalleled since the Reformation. This influence extends not only to many aspects of our national life but also to the life of churches and denominations. It is a sobering thought that many of the crucial discussions and heart-searchings we face as Protestant churches in this country at this hour have something or other to do with our attitude to the dogmas of the Roman Catholic Church. That is so whether one belongs to a church which is

Episcopalian, Presbyterian, Baptist or of some other denomination. It is a subject which we could ponder for a long time. But the fact is there and it must surely strike us as significant.

Our subject required that we should attempt to interpret the providence of God in history. Is there any one great practical issue to which such a survey draws particular attention? We believe that there is. The most urgent question of all for the present-day churches, in our considered opinion, is this: Were the old Protestant historians and theologians right to regard the Roman Catholic Church as no true church and to identify the Papacy with the Antichrist? Let us remember that they were, for the most part, men of profound erudition and spirituality— men such as Calvin, Owen, Turretin, Edwards, Cunningham and Charles Hodge. Let us further bear in mind that they claimed that their view of Rome was drawn from Scripture. Our reason for singling out this one issue is easily stated. The pre-twentieth-century Protestant church clung, by and large, to the anti-papal clauses in its creed. The present-day churches have, by and large, discarded them. The way Protestant churches view union with Rome is going to be momentously important from now on.

If the Catholic Church is not the Antichrist of Scripture as the old Protestant writers affirmed it to be, then there is ultimately no reason in principle why our Protestant churches should not return and reunite—if not this century, at least at some time in the future. But if the Reformers were right, then union with Rome is apostasy.

Precisely how and why Protestantism in this century came to hold a more relaxed attitude to Catholicism is one of the most intriguing, not to say burning, questions raised by the subject we have looked at. It would make a good theme for research. Indeed, it ought to compel the attention of every Protestant who takes seriously the events of this hour.

6

Our Need of Faith at This Hour

However we read the signs of the times these days, however we analyse the problems, wherever we place our own age within the prophetic calendar, one thing is certain: the modern Christian is called on to have faith in God above all else.

We are living today 'in a highly false moment of time'. That is the way Dr Edward Norman of Cambridge put it in his Reith Lectures. Christians mourn that as a civilization all our system of values seems to be standing on its head. The believer in the West is being bombarded by everything but outright persecution. Indeed the British Christian might, in certain respects, be worse off than some who are living in a police state. At any rate some Christians have evidently felt so, as the following account from only a few years ago might indicate: 'Despite the massive persecution of Christians in Russia, some families are returning from West Germany rather than remain in the constant barrage of erotic media material and sexual indulgence they found there.'[1] One bulwark of defence alone remains to the people of God at this hour. It is the vision of the throne of God seen by the psalmist: 'Thy throne is established of old; thou art from everlasting. The floods have lifted up, O Lord, the floods have lifted up their voice; the floods have lifted up their waves. The Lord on high is mightier than the noise of many waters, yea, than the mighty waves of the sea' [*Ps.* 93.2-4].

Faith is not merely the instrument of justification. It is the principle of the whole Christian life. 'We walk by faith,' says the apostle, meaning that we must never be influenced primarily by external events however much these alarm us. Nor must we go by feelings. If we do so we shall sink into hopeless discouragement. Never perhaps has it been more essential for believers to live by the light of Scripture than at this present time. What was said of Abraham must absolutely be true of us if we are to survive the storm: 'Who against hope believed in hope' [*Rom.* 4.18]. The marvellous power of faith is that it turns all that would otherwise discourage us into occasions of fresh hope and new confidence in the power of God. Had national sin and apostasy caused Judah to be 'trampled in a wine-press' by God? By faith Daniel made this very fact a stimulus to his own boldness before the throne of grace and an argument why God should now begin again to work in grace.

Do personal sins oppress us? By faith we must rise above the oppressing gloom, as William Bridge reminds us: 'If you would be truly humbled [i.e. for sin] and not be discouraged, not be discouraged and yet be humbled: then beat and drive up all your sins to your unbelief and lay the stress and weight of all your sorrow upon that sin.' [2]

WHAT IS FAITH?
The basic idea of faith is reliance. This is seen to be so in both the biblical languages, Hebrew and Greek. Faith is not just a nod of the head but a hearty acquiescence. There is no greater obedience possible to us than to believe, receive and then rest

upon the Word of God. To be able to believe is the highest expression of God's mercy. Hence it was that the great Dutch Remonstrant scholar, Grotius, said on his deathbed that he would gladly give up all his learning for the simple faith of his uneducated servant.

If our modern Calvinism is apt to differ at all from that of the palmy days of the past it is probably at this point. We emphasize knowledge; they stressed faith. We emphasize gifts; they insisted on grace. We study to inform the head; they studied to reform the heart. Our temptation is to neglect the soul—to fail in the cultivation of faith. The old books were strong where we are apt to be weak. *The Pilgrim's Progress* is all about progress in one thing—in faith. So too Doddridge's *The Rise and Progress of Religion in the Soul* and Romaine's *The Life, Walk and Triumph of Faith* are a sort of Mercator's map for the believer's soul.

It would be a thousand pities if Reformed Christians were to become, as some have already become, cerebral rather than spiritual. We all echo the dying words of J. Gresham Machen: 'Isn't the Reformed Faith grand!' Classic Calvinism of the Machen type has never permitted itself to indulge in spinning theological minuets or in constructing grandiose 'world-and-life' views divorced from the practical and eternal needs of ordinary men and women. Certainly Calvin would have nothing to do with a merely speculative faith. His definition of faith is aglow with realism: 'We shall now have a full definition of faith if we say that it is a firm and sure knowledge of the divine favour toward us, founded on the truth of a free promise in Christ, and revealed to our minds, and sealed on our hearts, by the Holy Spirit.'[3]

Faith is conviction of the truth of God. It rests on testimony. Hence older writers said that 'faith is human when it rests on the testimony of men; divine when it rests on the testimony of God' (Charles Hodge). Such sentiments find expression in all the standard theologians of the church, however far apart in other respects, from Aquinas to Owen and from Francis Turretin to John Howe.

That is why our great spiritual forefathers were pre-eminently men of one Book. They were not content till they could quote the Bible extensively and accurately, sing its psalms, expound its theology, apply its laws to daily life and solace themselves with it on their deathbeds.

MODERN LIFE AND UNBELIEF

The vices which immerse our unhappy generation were made inevitable by the nineteenth-century Higher Critical views of the Bible. Where there is no confident assertion by the church of the truth of God there can be no firm faith in the people. And where faith is absent every species of sin must sooner or later make its appearance. Our problem is that today sin has come to a monstrous ripeness. But the lineage is quite clear. Our drug addicts, our aborted infants, our sodomists and 'gay' people are the late fruits of the same tree of unbelief whose other branches included the Graf-Wellhausen theory, Jean Astruc and the 'Quest for the Historical Jesus'. To take away from the people an infallible Bible, as these did, was not just a sin; it was *the* sin, the very essence of all infidelity and of all irreligion. These earlier writers who laid the axe to the root of biblical infallibility did all in their power to banish heaven from earth and lay the world open to the unrestrained influences of hell itself.

But there is a subtler and more refined form of this assault on faith. It comes in the guise of learning and scholarship. It grants the existence of revealed truth and speaks the language of evangelicalism. But it attempts to gain credit for itself by such a show of learning that the sharp edge of truth is blunted and divine truths are made to speak with muted voice.

51

This is an age-old snare into which the church of Christ has fallen from time to time. For instance, the desire to conciliate the Greek secular mind led the Alexandrian Church Fathers to set out Christian truths in the dress of philosophy. The result was that the gospel was eventually transformed into a species of Platonic thought. What the Greek Fathers attempted the Schoolmen of the Middle Ages also set themselves to perfect—to prove the doctrines of the Christian faith philosophically. This was again done in Germany in the eighteenth century by Johann Christian Wolff, who set out to restate the Christian faith in terms of the philosophy of Leibniz. The same method of theologizing, perilous to faith, has been followed by prominent religious thinkers from Schleiermacher to Karl Barth and from Rudolf Bultmann to John Macquarrie. According to Bultmann the Bible is 'written within the framework of an ancient and now incredible world-view'. Such are the learned weapons used to murder the faith of men.

THE BENEFITS OF FAITH

Reformed preachers in the world today are faced with the daunting task of starting to rebuild the faith of nations almost from scratch. Gone, at least in Britain, are the vast Nonconformist congregations of the past, whether Congregational, Baptist or Presbyterian. But one thing remains: our faith in the trustworthiness of God, whose Word cannot lie.

The great call of the hour is surely to become men of far sturdier faith than we have yet attained to. The examples of such men of faith as Edwards, whose youthful 'Resolutions' shaped his whole life and ministry, and Flavel, with his experience of the nearness of God to the believing soul, are a standing reminder to us at this hour that the most useful ministries are those most full of faith, expectation of blessing and felt enjoyment of his presence. Signs may not be lacking that a better day lies ahead. O, that we might find grace to spend and be spent for the sake of Christ's cause in our difficult day so that we might obtain a similar commendation to that of the great old 'apostle' to the northern counties of England, Bernard Gilpin: 'He was careful to avoid not only all evil doing, but even the slightest suspicions thereof. And he was accounted a saint in the judgments of his very enemies, if he had any such. Being full of faith unfeigned, and of good works, he was at last put into his grave as a heap of wheat in due time swept into the garner.'[4] That would be an epitaph worth labouring for!

II

Fellowship With Christ

Behold, I stand at the door, and knock:
if any man hear my voice,
and open the door,
I will come in to him,
and will sup with him,
and he with me.

Revelation 3:20.

7
Christ the Lover of Our Souls

Ecstasy and delight are essential to the believer's soul and they promote sanctification. We were not meant to live without spiritual exhilaration and the Christian who goes for a long time without the experience of heart-warming will soon find himself tempted to have his emotions satisfied from earthly things and not, as he ought, from the Spirit of God. The soul is so constituted that it craves fulfilment from things outside itself and will embrace earthly joys for satisfaction when it cannot reach spiritual ones. Not for nothing did Satan draw Eve to see that the forbidden fruit grew on a tree which was 'pleasant to the eyes' and on a 'tree to be desired'. The believer is in spiritual danger if he allows himself to go for any length of time without tasting the love of Christ and savouring the felt comforts of a Saviour's presence. When Christ ceases to fill the heart with satisfaction, our souls will go in silent search of other lovers.

It is not altogether an easy task to say what enjoyment of Christ consists of and perhaps it would be best to start with the negative aspects of the subject. By spiritual elevation we do not have in mind simply the social joys which Christians have in company with one another. These are both real and very necessary, but they are not all that is referred to here under the theme of the enjoyment of God in the gospel. Neither do we refer to the boisterous movement of the arms which in some circles appears to be deemed essential to public worship. Again, we do not have any thought here of that grotesque medieval 'enjoyment' of Christ indulged in by certain nuns who claimed to hold with Christ a sort of spiritual flirtation, as their recorded meditations show.

By the enjoyment of the love of Christ in the heart of a believer we mean an experience of the 'love of God shed abroad in our hearts by the Holy Ghost which is given unto us' [Rom. 5:5]. It is impossible to deny that this is an actual experience. It is not that we are conscious of our own love to God but that we are made wonderfully aware of his love to us. This text is to be understood as referring to an emotion registered in the consciousness of a true believer and resulting from the impression upon his human spirit of the love which God bears to him in Christ. The love of God is something which is always there towards the believer but he may not be always aware of it. Because the Lord has made himself accessible to us in the means of grace, it is our duty and privilege to seek this experience from him in these means till we are made the joyful partakers of it.

Once a believer has tasted this love of God in his soul he can never rest content till he has it again and again. The biblical enjoyment of the grace of Christ is not to be looked on as abnormal or extraordinary but as part of his earthly inheritance. It is for this reason that the apostle Paul can refer to the Holy Spirit as the 'earnest of our inheritance' [Eph. 1:14]. The 'earnest' is more than the pledge or guarantee. It is the first part or the initial payment in kind. There can be no reasonable doubt that this is the meaning of the term 'earnest' in the Word of God. It denotes experience and cannot be confined to what is merely doctrinal or theoretical. Put simply, it indicates that in the teaching of the apostles there is an enjoyment of God which is to be expected and to be looked for. There are gracious communications made to us in this life. The Spirit is the agent who generates a felt joy and exhilaration in the consciousness of the child of God.

It would be misleading to imagine that this experience of the love of Christ is a thing confined to the New Testament. It may well be and very probably is true that there is a fuller measure of this religious ecstasy poured in to the hearts of New Testament saints than before the work of Christ was completed on the cross. That would be consistent with the greater fullness associated with our age as the 'last times'. But there is a wealth of evidence to show that the Old Testament saints were very well aware of this inward enjoyment of God in the means of grace. What else is meant by the psalmist when he refers to God as 'God my exceeding joy' [Ps. 43:4]? When he tells the Lord that he is the 'health of his countenance' he means to say that his face, reflecting his inward mood of dejection, is cast down with sorrow whenever he is unable to go to the house of the Lord to enjoy God in the means of grace.

The psalmist speaks of God in terms which indicate clearly enough to us that he was in the habit of feeling an inward sensation of gladness and even ecstasy when the Spirit was poured out on his heart. To this effect are the many passages which say that we are to 'taste' the goodness of God [Ps. 34:8]; that we are to 'pant' after him, 'thirst' for him, 'appear before him' and enjoy his 'lovingkindness'. All of which terms occur in this same psalm and indicate that the godly man is authorized to expect much more from God in this life than merely an enjoyment of him which is the result of *mental* understanding. Indeed, there are evidences in plenty that both in the Old and New Testament periods of the church the true people of God knew the heartwarming experiences of which we are speaking as they met publicly in the sanctuary. To this effect is Psalm 63, among others, where the psalmist speaks of 'seeing thy power and thy glory so as I have seen thee in the sanctuary' and at once talks of having his soul 'satisfied as with marrow and fatness' and as rejoicing 'in the shadow of thy wings' [Ps. 63:2,5,7]. Nothing other than the felt enjoyment of the love of God in his heart could compel him to declare: 'thy lovingkindness is better than life' [v.3]. On the other hand he falls into the deepest gloom and despondency whenever he is in circumstances which make it impossible to know this love of God in the gospel. So he cries out, 'Woe is me that I sojourn in Mesech!' [Ps. 120:5].

How different all this is from those formalized and predictable religious exclamations which so often pass for piety and are no more the true sentiments of the heart than the sounding of brass or the clanging of a cymbal! How offensive to a God of knowledge must those repeated and reiterated utterances be which sound out so monotonously with 'amen' and 'hallelujah' and are as devoid of felt inward enjoyment of God's love as a record when the needle sticks in the grooves! By all means let the believer tell out what he feels but let him not insult God by attempting to spice his often cold and ignorant devotions with sacred ejaculations which he does not really mean. True excitement in the worship of God is not something which can be generated by flexing the vocal chords. It is a travesty to repeat over-worked exclamations or to parrot religious phraseology so as to sound pious. The worshipper who comes to God to get a felt blessing does well, but he must go about the task in a right manner and not think to work himself up into the love of God as though he were an athlete warming up on the track or a dervish lashing himself into a state of frenzy.

We are brought, then, to the important question as to how the believer goes about the work of finding the felt blessing. This is a spiritual art in itself and yet it is something we may learn from the Word of truth like any other aspect of our faith.

HOW DO WE GO TO GOD FOR A SENSE OF HIS LOVE?
The way to get God's felt blessing on our hearts begins with an act of faith. That is to say we must believe that there is such a thing to be had in this life. If we do not expect or even believe in such experiences, the probability is that we shall know but little of them. If it is part of our imagined wisdom to scoff at religious experiences as such and to smile condescendingly when we hear devout men tell of their enjoyment of God in the means of grace, we are guilty of quenching the Spirit and are not coming in a hopeful or promising way to the throne of grace. By all means let us be dismissive of spurious and unwarranted experience. But there is, as we have sought to show, a true and scriptural enjoyment of Christ which is no fanaticism but the subjective fruit of the gospel.

Then, having become convinced that there is a genuine experience of a 'felt Christ' to be had on earth, we must go to God in prayer for it. The blessings of the covenant of grace are to be had by believing prayer and the principle holds good in this case also. We come to the throne of grace as suppliants to receive this choice favour of 'tasting', or being made subjectively conscious of the love God has to us in Christ.

It is the view of the present writer that we often go astray at this point. It is the way of many to begin in prayer with strong affirmations of their love to God. But let us be careful. It is our personal belief that we would start off more promisingly if we began the other way round, that is, by admitting how very little we love God. The secret of getting the blessing from God is to put ourselves down as far as possible and to put him up as high as possible. In effect, therefore, we do well to start our prayer for the felt presence of his love by telling the Lord, not how much we love him, but how piteously little. Admittedly we cannot restrict prayer to a formula or to a routine of words of any sort, but we do need to begin always by taking a lowly place at his feet whenever we come to him and desire a blessing, as we ought at all times to do. It is our folly to become habituated to praying without any sense of God's power upon our hearts. We do harm to our souls and hinder our own progress in the knowledge of God if we treat prayer as an exercise of the mind only and do not expect to emerge from the presence of God with a fresh token of his love borne in upon us. It is a mistake to pray with our mouths alone or even with our gifts alone. Fluency is a good thing but it is not the highest form of prayer. In true prayer there is a concurrence of man's spirit with the Spirit of God. The Spirit assists us 'with groanings which cannot be uttered'. These are felt by the worshipper and are the birth-pangs which precede the blessing.

The dreadful possibility is that we learn to copy the prayers of those who are irreverent, for some people approach God in terms which are appropriate to an equal but which are entirely out of place in approaching the sublime Deity. We shall not know much enjoyment of God's rich favour till we have learned to talk to the Almighty in other tones of voice and with lower levels of self-abasement than those appropriate in human company. God expects us to treat him with becoming awe and shamefacedness. The irreverent prayer is atrocious because it is a contradiction in terms. Prayer is by definition a treating of God as his majesty demands.

At the same time there is a fault frequently found of an opposite kind. We are not to talk to God 'politely'. It is one of the many remarkable things about the prayers recorded in the Scriptures that they are reverent but not 'polite'. That is to say, God does not expect us to talk to him according to the codes of human etiquette. The 'please and thank you' state of mind is not that of the great men of prayer in the Word of God. We are, rather, to 'take hold of him' and wrestle with him as Jacob did. We are to cast ourselves down at his feet and then to make mighty demands upon him, like men in such deadly earnest to get his blessing that they would expire at his feet in an agony of effort if they did not succeed with him.

God does not, it seems to us, frequently yield up his blessing to us till we have spent a reasonable length of time in his presence. Concentration demands the quiet, steady settling of our minds upon God as we pray. We should learn to be with him for some considerable time if we are in earnest for the felt presence. Even then there will be many times when we shall rise from our knees with disappointment that we did not feel such a sense of felt blessing as we yearned to have. At other times, however, those who seek the face of the Lord in downright earnest will rise up from the secret place with a 'joy unspeakable' and with an impression of Christ's love on their hearts which is unforgettable.

There is, however, the very real possibility in every Christian that he will learn to live at a distance from the love of Christ. Our corruption works in us a constant tendency to withdraw from Christ into the shadows. Days and even months can go past in the experience of the Lord's people in which they are virtual strangers to the inward enjoyment of the love of Christ in their hearts. The soul grows callous. Layers of worldliness or coldness, like coats of paint on an old door, overspread the soul till we become accustomed to feeling nothing, enjoying nothing, expecting nothing, knowing nothing of those heart-warmings which are all-important to spiritual well-being. The next step is that the believer falls into a dead formalism. Prayer is got through as mere duty and routine. The Bible is read either to keep up appearances or to salve the weak voice of conscience. But spiritual exercises are now no longer enjoyed. The soul has no relish for the things of the Spirit. The consequence is that new companions are sought who are unfriendly to heart-religion. Then corners are cut in obedience to the Word of God. Finally, offence is taken at the lives of those Christians in the fellowship who are walking with God in 'the power of godliness'. These are now criticised by the cold Christian as 'too narrow', 'too strict', 'carrying things too far', 'extremists', 'trouble-makers', and then, at last, 'not really belonging to our church' because they are 'old fashioned' or 'bigoted'.

Countless believers have declined in this way. Part of the tragedy is that they have fallen into coldness while convincing themselves that they were serving God. The scholar at his books persuades himself that he is too busy to spend an hour each morning in secret devotions. The pastor feels he cannot devote time to the cultivation of his soul because he has too many letters to reply to or even sermons to prepare. The missionary cannot wait on the Lord as he used to because of the pressures of language-study, and later on, because of daily duties at the mission, and later on still, because of deputation work in the home country.

In these crafty ways does the devil lead God's people by a staircase which winds ever downwards. But let us recall in the midst of our busy life that we may do ourselves and the cause of God great harm by our neglect of the soul. Let us once lose the dew of our spiritual freshness and we are at once a ready prey to compromise. How have so many evils come into the church but through men's neglecting to cultivate daily fellowship with Christ? Like the Ephesian church in the Book of Revelation, they have been busily engaged in their 'works' and 'labour' and 'patience' and even their zeal for orthodoxy. But in the eyes of the

Saviour they have 'left their first love' [*Rev.* 2:2-4] and risk losing the very 'candlestick' altogether.

Even so today it is fearfully possible for a believer to be heavily involved in the fight against ecumenism or secularism or a thousand other evil things and yet to lose the tone and edge of his spirituality. But what does the Lord require of us? Is it not that we should walk close to him? Let no one imagine that the spending of much time conscientiously in daily fellowship with Christ will result in loss of service. Time spent with God in the secret place is never the cause of spiritual inefficiency. On the contrary, it is the highway to fresh vision and to new triumphs. 'To have prayed well is to have studied well.' This motto was Luther's and announces to us the secret of his immense labours and abounding faithfulness.

We may conclude as we began, with a concern to revive in ourselves and in our brethren far more emphasis on heart-religion. As we view the state of the churches, this is the great priority everywhere. Nothing must be permitted to weaken our cultivation of fellowship with Christ. If one day's schedule is too full to allow us much time for secret prayer, then the next day must be made to yield more time for it as a compensation. Outward duties need themselves to be remoulded in our lives so as to become means of fellowship with God. What yields no spiritual profit at all to us in the course of life needs in all probability to be pruned out from our daily agenda altogether. The overwhelming concern of the Christian's life must surely be to live unto God, upon God and for God. What else can the familiar words mean where the apostle Paul tells us, 'For to me to live is Christ'?

What a force for good even a handful of Christians would be who lived in near intimacy with the Lord Jesus Christ! What prayers would be heard again in the earth as believers took hold of the sleeve of Christ and drew down the blessing! What power and authority for our preaching would flow out of his glorious 'fulness' [*John* 1:16]! What new life would be breathed into all our meetings if an army of M'Cheynes emerged from their closets melted with gospel-love! What new levels of excitement would there be in our services if preachers came into their pulpits clothed in the garments of visible holiness! In a word, what might not be done for God if only we were not so ignorant of him!

It is to be feared that our gospel suffers today because our credibility is low. If the enemies of our message could but discern in us a greater likeness to our Lord and Master they would at least listen to us more carefully, even if they would not believe our message. But where else is this credibility to come from except as we resolve to hold closer communion with the Lord himself? And how else are we to obtain a desire to hold this communion with him except as we learn to have our souls daily more filled with his Spirit? We are not yet 'Reformed' in the best sense of that term till we excel in that experience of fellowship with Christ which made Knox's prayers more potent than an army.

Perhaps there is no more fitting illustration in our biographical literature of the theme we speak of than the experience of John Welsh on his deathbed. According to Robert Fleming's account, Welsh was so overcome with the felt enjoyment of God that he was sometimes overheard in prayer to say these words: 'Lord, hold thy hand; it is enough. Thy servant is a clay vessel and can hold no more.' [1]

8

'Better Than Wine'

When the bride in the Song of Solomon wished to experience afresh the love of her beloved, she exclaimed: 'Let him kiss me with the kisses of his mouth: for thy love is better than wine' [1:2]. No words could more perfectly express the longings of the Christian's soul for new and refreshing enjoyment of the love of Christ. Every true believer echoes the sentiment that the love of Jesus is 'better than wine'. As wine fills the mouth with the taste of sweetness, so does Christ fill the heart of the child of God. As wine refreshes and gladdens the spirit of man, so does a taste of Christ's love elevate and exhilarate the Christian's soul. As wine banishes care and brings ease to the heart and mirth to the lips, so does the love of Jesus lift the believer's mind above earthly care and stir within him strong emotions of delight in God. But, whereas wine may cheer man only for a time and may then leave him weakened and worsened by intoxication, the love of Christ is a never-failing tonic which puts iron into the soul and makes a man 'beside himself ' [2 Cor. 5:13] only in a way that honours God.

This theme of a believer's enjoyment of Christ's love is a frequent one in the Holy Scriptures and yet, strangely, it is one which we may so easily overlook. At least, we may so far overlook it as to take only a theoretical interest in it as a mere item of theology for which we make a space in our minds but of which we have only a scanty experience in our hearts. But for the Christian to treat the love of Christ as a mere item on the agenda of his theology is to run the risk of offending the Lord and starving his own soul of vital spiritual nourishment. There are, therefore, compelling reasons why every Christian should pause frequently in life and ask himself if, amidst all the duties of his calling, he has a felt enjoyment of the love of Christ in his heart or whether, amid the welter of his conflicts and strivings, he ought honestly to confess to himself and to the Lord that he has left his 'first love' [*Rev.* 2:4].

A MATTER OF PRIORITIES

The Christian's life is seldom lived out in the rarefied atmosphere of an ivory tower. The pressures of a sinful world bear in upon us almost ceaselessly day and night. Our own hearts are a tinder-box of latent mischief and corruption. In addition, Satan untiringly plies his trade of seduction, casting into our minds his 'fiery darts' [*Eph.* 6:16] in order to kindle and keep burning the flammable material within us and so to roast us pitilessly in the fires of our own depravity, if he can. Almost all a Christian sees is a burden and a trial to him. The state of society is a grief to his mind; the present earthly condition of the church is a fruitful source of care to him; the whole world and all within it is a daily reminder to him that 'all things are full of labour; man cannot utter it' [*Eccles.* 1:8] and that 'all is vanity and vexation of spirit' [*Eccles.* 1:14]. Clearly, we live in a world where 'that which is crooked cannot be made straight: and that which is wanting (or lacking) cannot be numbered' [v.15].

Nothing we do (and we ought to do everything in our power) can fully negate the effects of sin or wholly reverse the sentence of 'vanity' pronounced by God upon the entire world [*Rom.*

8:20]. Exert ourselves as we may in church and state to lift things back to God, pray and labour as we can to have Christ's kingdom advanced, we know as a matter of principle that we shall never silence the groanings within us [*Rom.* 8:23] for a rejuvenated universe till the Lord himself comes the second time.

In the light of these facts, both of Scripture and of experience, we are apt on occasion, as Christians, to become almost swallowed up with conflicts, activities and burdensome cares. Certainly, there is no avoiding these inconveniences if we mean to be faithful to Christ. It would never be right for us to withdraw from the sphere of God's calling or to throw down our arms and flee from the field of battle. But, on the other hand, we must not allow ourselves to be pressurized by circumstances in such a way that we lose sight of our priorities.

There is no priority higher in the believer's life than to delight himself in the love of Christ. When our circumstances have succeeded in crowding out a sense of the love which Christ bears towards us, then we have allowed ourselves to be pressurized into a false position where we are in danger. This lesson comes home to us from many passages of Scripture. Psalm 73 is a notable instance. Asaph allowed his circumstances and his thoughts to lead him away from his priorities for a time. That is the great theme of this famous and helpful psalm. So long as he forgot the love of God towards believers, Asaph was in danger of being bitter, cynical and envious of the wicked. But as soon as he came to himself and remembered the love which God bears to his own people and to them only, he ceased to 'slip' [v.2] and was able to go on his way with his triumphant song: 'Whom have I in heaven but thee? and there is none upon earth that I desire beside thee. My flesh and my heart faileth: but God is the strength of my heart, and my portion for ever' [*Ps.* 73:25-26].

The very same emphasis on the love of Christ is to be found

in the apostle Paul also. What minister (indeed, what Christian) was ever in greater danger of being engulfed with work and care than Paul? Whoever in Christian history could record a longer catalogue than Paul of imprisonments, labours, journeyings, sufferings or tribulation? And yet there is always in Paul's writings a warm consciousness of the love of Christ.

The epistles of Paul are a standing reminder to the people of God that we must never lose our sense of priorities. In the midst of all the fierce invective and the unanswerable theologizing of his letter to the Galatians, Paul finds space to refer to 'the Son of God, who loved me, and gave himself for me' [2:20], is at pains to remind us that 'the fruit of the Spirit is love' [5:22] and concludes with the reminder that the marks in his body are 'the marks of the Lord Jesus' [6:17].

Similarly, in writing to the Ephesians as 'the prisoner of the Lord' [4:1] he announces to his readers that the highest aspiration of his soul for them is that they might 'be able to comprehend with all saints what is the breadth, and length, and depth, and height; and to know the love of Christ, which passeth knowledge' [3:18-19]. To the Philippians, again writing from prison, he is at pains early in his letter to state that for him 'to live is Christ' [1:21]; and before he ends his diatribe against 'dogs . . . evil workers . . . [and] the concision' [3:2], he cannot hide from his readers his own personal ambition, which is to attain 'the prize of the high calling of God in Christ Jesus' [3:14]. This is the spirit of Paul in all his epistles, and in that he bids us to take himself as our model [*1 Cor.* 11:1, *Phil.* 3:17], it is our clear duty to preserve the same priority as he had in the Christian life.

THE PLACE OF SANCTIFIED EMOTIONS
There is another reason why every Christian needs to dwell long and often on the theme of Christ's love and to drink deeply from

that 'cup of salvation' [Ps. 116:13]. It is because we need to enjoy the sanctified and sanctifying emotions which an experience of the love of Christ gives to us.

It is undeniably true that a very great deal that is worthless has been said and written over the centuries of the church's history about experience. But we would be foolish to ignore entirely the place of emotion in the Christian life. There is such a thing as 'tasting that the Lord is gracious' [1 Pet. 2:3] and tasting is more than notion. Emotions of delight, peace, comfort and reassurance are as surely and certainly a part of authentic Christian experience as the emotions of fear and anguish generally are of the unregenerate, yet awakened, sinner.

Perhaps, as a generation of Christians, we fall short in this point more than most others, that we are often emotionally stunted, even when our minds are well furnished with divinity. But if we wish to grow in spiritual profundity we would do well to covet more those emotions which the New Testament presents to us as normal and healthful to the believer: 'joy in the Holy Ghost' [Rom. 14:17], 'the love of God shed abroad in our hearts by the Holy Ghost' [Rom. 5:5], 'the peace of God, which passeth all understanding' [Phil. 4:7], 'joy unspeakable and full of glory' [1 Pet. 1:8], and whatsoever else are represented to us in God's Word as Spirit-given emotions. Whilst we rightly recoil from sentimentality and hollow expressions of Christian emotion, we must beware not to react so strongly that we become afraid of what is genuine and even inevitable.

Genuine emotion in the Christian is sometimes the fruit of his own meditation on the theology which he believes. Sometimes too it is the result of something still more profound and mysterious, the action of God's Spirit upon our spirit [Rom. 8:15-16, 23, 26, 2 Cor. 5:4-5, Rom. 5:5; 14:17].

It is all too possible for us to read the Puritans and not to notice that they were a race of Christians who not only thought clearly about, but also felt strongly, the truths of the gospel. Their 'day-books', diaries and other autobiographical remains reveal to us a people who were deeply exercised in soul. They were no strangers to sighs, tears, groans, spiritual elevation, heavenly foretastes and periodic ecstasies. If we had nothing to go by but only Bunyan's *Pilgrim's Progress* we should have evidence enough to make good our case that they were a deeply feeling, deeply exercised generation of believers who would have found a cerebral, unfeeling Christianity unrecognizable.

When all due allowance is made for the difference between one Christian's temperament and another's, we must surely come back to this, that the more we appreciate the love of Christ towards us, the more comfort we shall have along the way to glory. Christ has loved us 'with an everlasting love' [*Jer.* 31:3]. He has in love given himself for us to be 'a propitiation for our sins' [*1 John* 4:10]. Very soon we shall see him in his glory and enjoy his love eternally. It is therefore only fitting that here and now we should seek from God a frequent enjoyment of that love. He who experiences it will both renew his strength and reinvigorate his soul. In so doing, he will find that the love of Jesus is 'better than wine'.

9
The Christian's Refreshing

It is a part of the Christian's experience to come to seasons of rest and refreshing. These are as important for the soul as times of labour and tribulation, but they seem less frequent. In this way God varies the experiences of the pilgrim journey for each of his children, so that they always have some way of escape from their temptations and some seasons of rest from the burden and heat of the day.

In the journey to Canaan, relief was given to Israel periodically, by the discovery of some fresh oasis or welcome provision of water. In the same way, the Lord's people, on their journey to Zion today, are refreshed as they are led by Christ to new sources of comfort. God brings his weary servants over the trackless wastes of their desert wanderings by stages. From time to time they are rested and refreshed at an oasis of mercy. At such times, it is as if the Lord were saying, 'This is the rest . . . and this is the refreshing' [*Isa.* 28:12].

The comfort of these experiences to the weary Christian's soul is exquisite. The mirage becomes a pool and 'the thirsty land springs of water' [*Isa.* 35:7]. God commands the traveller to be still, to come apart and rest from the storm of spiritual conflict. The believer stops for a while and pauses to drink deep draughts of comfort. Such moments are highly welcome. They are sometimes unforgettable. They regale the spirit of man at the time they are enjoyed and they return to his mind in later years, when the recollection of them is still sweet and exhilarating.

PHYSICAL REST

There are times in the Christian's life when he must recognize and accept that he is in need of a thorough rest. Every faculty in the man of God is engaged in the spiritual warfare. It is therefore not surprising that every faculty becomes periodically exhausted. The body and mind become jaded and the spirit feels no longer able to rise up in hope. When God's servants have laboured and toiled for months together at the post of duty (whether the duty be secular or spiritual) and come to the point of chronic fatigue, they need not feel ashamed to obey the call of a tired constitution. They must unwind and relax. Life without proper relaxation loses its delight and becomes a drudgery. No man can give of his best when he is worn down and spent.

We are apt to think the work of God will collapse if we do not hold it up continually with all our might. But if we think that, we have forgotten who God is. The work of God existed and prospered on earth before we were born. It will also exist and prosper when we are dead and forgotten. Scarcely any greater affront could be offered to God than that odious sentiment of liberal theology which imagines that 'God has no other hands and feet than ours'. On the contrary, his 'chariots are twenty thousand' [Ps. 68:17]. Heaven and earth could more easily pass away than the church of Christ. Concerning the church, God says, 'I the Lord do keep it; I will water it every moment; lest any hurt it, I will keep it night and day' [Isa 27:3]. 'He that keepeth Israel shall neither slumber nor sleep' [Ps. 121:4].

The Lord Jesus Christ was not ashamed to be found asleep in the boat [Mark 4:38]. His people therefore do not need to feel

ashamed when, after exhausting service, they too must yield their
aching bodies to a period of necessary rest.

WHEN REFRESHMENT IS ESSENTIAL

There are some who profess faith in Christ who scarcely know
what a hard day's work in his service means. For them, one day
is much like another. Their agenda of life is about pleasing oneself. They have never learnt how to serve others by love. It is not
for these that the refreshment we speak of is designed by the
Master. But it is for those who pour themselves out unceasingly
in doing good. It is for those who mourn for the afflictions of
Zion, who fight the good fight and whose care is to 'build the
walls of Jerusalem' [*Ps.* 51:18].

The conscientious Christian, on the other hand, is inclined to
overwork himself. In his dutiful opinion, it is *never* the right time
to rest. Though his wife and family counsel him to take a much-
needed time of relaxation, he argues himself into a redoubling of
his efforts. Though his close friends hint kindly that his work
would be the better if he were to take a week or two of rest, he
lashes himself to undertake an additional load of Christian activity. Such heroes still grace the church of Christ even in these
days. The people of God should take their hats off to them. They
are worth their weight in gold. But they are not above friendly
criticism. There are times when rest is essential.

There are certain warning signs which should tell us that we
need to relax and to unwind. One such sign is when our mind
becomes incapable of facing any aspect of our work with pleasure. There are many aspects of our work, of course, which we
would all prefer not to have to face. That is normal enough. But
there is a state of mind to which tired people come, in which
everything they do looks like a fresh sentence in purgatory.
When all the joy has gone from our work, it is usually a sign that

the time has come to rest. Again, when all spiritual exercises become wearisome and we can face prayer or preaching only by dragging ourselves to them, it is a sign that rest and relaxation are essential. When we inwardly fight with all the world and all our thoughts turn into battles, it is a sign that nature is over-stretched. When we feel that death is our only comfort, that the light of the sun is only darkness and the prospect of tomorrow is a nightmare, then it is a pointer to the need for a time of respite. When Christ seems to be a harsh Master and the prom-ises of Scripture to be hollow, then it is time to draw aside and seek a season of quietness. Scientists have learnt, by disasters in aircraft, that fatigue occurs even in metal. How much more does man's frail body, which is a house of clay, suffer from fatigue!

CONSCIENTIOUS OBJECTIONS

It is no easy task to persuade a hard-worked Christian that overworking is not a virtue. 'I have no time to rest,' says one man. But a nervous breakdown may force him to find time for rest. It would be wiser and better to stop for a while before the nervous system becomes overloaded, rather than afterwards. 'I am called on to fight,' says another man. But every soldier needs a time away from the dust and heat of battle. 'There is time enough to rest in heaven,' exclaims a third man. True, but the quality of our work on earth is impaired if we go about it always with a tired mind. Perhaps we have forgotten that: 'Except the Lord build the house, they labour in vain that build it: except the Lord keep the city, the watchman waketh but in vain. It is vain for you to rise up early, to sit up late, to eat the bread of sorrows: for so he giveth his beloved sleep' [Ps. 127:1-2]

REFRESHMENT OF SOUL

It is a mistake to equate rest with idleness. The believer will welcome rest, not so much for its own sake, but because it is the most efficient way to prepare himself for further service for the Lord Jesus Christ. Rest, after all, is the best preparation for work. So far, we have referred mainly to that bodily rest which we associate with times of holiday. But there is a type of refreshment available to the Christian which reaches beyond the material side of life and touches the very soul. It is this which is the most significant aspect of our theme and the one which we most need to experience in these days in which we live.

The initiation into spiritual rest comes to a man when he becomes assured of his good standing in Christ. Hence our Saviour declares, 'Ye shall find rest unto your souls' [*Matt.* 11:29]. But it would not be true to say that the believer never stands in need of any further refreshing in his soul once he receives this assurance. The reverse is clearly the case. Christians need to be refreshed again and again. This is an aspect of the believer's life which probably does not receive the attention it deserves.

The apostle Paul refers at several points in his epistles to the subject of spiritual refreshment. He says that he looked forward to a time of refreshment when he would share fellowship with believers at Rome [*Rom.* 15:32]. He tells us that he was refreshed by brethren from Corinth who ministered to him [*1 Cor.* 16:18], and declares that Titus' soul had been refreshed also at Corinth [*2 Cor.* 7:13]. He commends Philemon for refreshing the hearts of God's people [*Philem.* 7] and marks out Onesiphorus for special mention as one who had often refreshed him during his time of imprisonment [*2 Tim.* 1:16]. The experience Paul speaks of is clearly a spiritual one, open to us all to seek. It is that cheering and heart-warming sensation in the soul by which we feel lifted above life's storms and cares to a sense of eternal things. This refreshing may be experienced in fellowship with believers or it may come secretly to the heart by means of a sermon, a book or a time of prayer.

The refreshment of which we speak is a renewed enjoyment of God in Christ. It is vital to the life of the soul to receive such impressions of blessing from time to time. By invisible influences and mysterious agencies, God communicates fresh supplies of divine comfort to us at such a season. By their means the heart of the Christian, formerly bent low with care, is once more lifted up with 'joy unspeakable and full of glory' [1 Pet. 1:8]. 'Be still and know that I am God' [Ps. 46:10] is, as it were, breathed like a message from heaven into the troubled heart. The ripples of life are calmed once again and the storm in the mind is soothed into a state of peace. The experienced believer recognizes in this experience the voice of Christ and he takes comfort.

The diaries and journals of great Christians do not lack their references to this experience of spiritual refreshment. In prisons, on lonely mission fields, amidst a thousand cares and toils, on beds of sickness, at their journey's end, God's people have sought and found the presence of Christ in a way that has refreshed and renewed them in heart, when all else on earth has failed.

We in our feverish world, perhaps more than those before us, need to wait on Christ for this comfort and enlivenment of soul. Let us apply frequently to him for it, for our own good and the good of others. 'This is the rest wherewith ye may cause the weary to rest, and this is the refreshing' [Isa. 28:12].

10

The Surpassing Love of Christ

Perhaps nothing is more surprising in all creation than the love of Christ to his people. Our familiarity with the many passages of Scripture which refer to it sometimes makes us insensitive to the amazing magnitude of it. Words are strangely double-edged things. The more frequently we read them the less power over us they tend to have. Consequently we are always in danger of gliding over great doctrines unthinkingly and unfeelingly because we learn so quickly the deplorable habit of passing those doctrines rapidly through the mind as matters which we take for granted.

It is unquestionably one of the tragic fruits of our fallen nature that we can grow in theological knowledge without growing perceptibly in appreciation of what that knowledge means. The head may be full, while the heart is cold. Truths may be handled clinically without the affections becoming roused or kindled. Indeed, the oftener we study any doctrine the less sweetness it seems to give us. This would surely not be so if sin were not our ruin. But as we are in this life, the law of diminishing returns spoils our appreciation of even the choicest truths we profess.

Could any news be more exquisitely welcome than that God should love any man? There is frequent clamour among men for good news. It is obvious to them that *good* news is rare in this world. Of bad news there is plenty and men hear it daily to the point of nausea. The saying of Christ 'sufficient unto the day is the evil thereof' [*Matt.* 6:34] has its relevance to the torrent of bad news we hear and have to hear each day. Rare are the days of our life which do not bring us painful news of 'wars and rumours of wars', of famine and earthquakes, of crime and covetousness, of theft, murder and violence. But good news is a very scarce commodity upon earth.

The Bible's message to us involves the breathtakingly good news that 'God is love'. Such a statement, were we not made of stone, would be so welcome to us in this dark world of misery that we should run to trumpet it from the housetops. Only our chronic deafness makes us so unresponsive to such transcendentally glad tidings. But we must school ourselves to listen more carefully to this mighty piece of information. When we still our minds to hear the good news of God's love, it beggars all our thoughts and swallows up all our fears. If God is love then every anxiety of believers is a lie. Over all the carnage of war and above the ghastly spectacle of human woe, over every helmet of the warrior and garment rolled in blood there is the rainbow of God's covenanted grace. There is meaning to the most random events in life. There is a benign and wise Father in, through and over all things, even things filled with pain, suffering and death.

There would be comfort in the thought of God's kindness even if such kindness were pity and nothing more. It would be comfort of a kind to think of there being compassion in God even if nothing more were meant than that God pities man's plight but is powerless to prevent it. If this were all the Bible taught, it would fall far short of the ideal. But it would be worth something to an agonized humanity to look up amid the pangs and death-throes of our predicament and to know that above the clouds sat a spectator-God who cared about, even if he could not cure, our maladies. For it is something to the wretched to know even of helpless onlookers who have sympathy and compassion.

But, blessed be God, our condition is inconceivably better than the case we have just imagined. The reality is that the God who pities both can, and wishes to, lift man above his miseries on earth. More still, he *has* acted in history, in the person of his Son Jesus Christ, in just such a way as to solve every problem, lift every burden, unloose every bond and remove every misery when we come trustingly to him. It is to rouse our witless minds to some appreciation of the immensity of God's grace in the gospel that the prophets write in a style of seeming hyperbole: 'Sing, O heavens; and be joyful, O earth; and break forth into singing, O mountains: for the Lord hath comforted his people, and will have mercy upon his afflicted' [*Isa.* 49:13]. 'Let the heavens rejoice, and let the earth be glad; let the sea roar, and the fulness thereof. Let the field be joyful, and all that is therein: then shall the trees of the wood rejoice before the Lord; for he cometh, for he cometh to judge the earth: he shall judge the world with righteousness, and the people with his truth' [*Ps.* 96:11-13].

Why else should these inspired writers call on inanimate nature to leap up in a chorus of song except to surprise us out of our inattention to the great goodness of God towards us in the gospel? Knowing our minds to be nine-tenths asleep to God's love, therefore, they aim to startle us from our lack of appreciation by calling on all nature, as it were, to sound a cannonade.

Where shall we begin if we are to speak of the love of Christ? In marvellous kindness to us he looked past the fallen angels, leaving them irrevocably in their sins, and laid hold of mankind, who were far lower in the scale of created excellence. Let no one suppose Christ to have *needed* our love, our fellowship or our devotion. As God he was eternally sufficient unto himself, and as the Son of God he knew eternally the ineffable fellowship of the Father and of the Spirit. When therefore he stooped to clothe himself with our weak humanity, he undertook an action of such philanthropy that the whole angelic world must have gasped and stilled its wings in breathless adoration. O the love of a Christ who fills heaven and earth, yet puts on the garment of my manhood to bless me in himself!

But let us see Christ in his life on earth, the holy and great God-Man, 'trailing clouds of glory' from the cradle to the cross. How patiently he bears with the 'contradiction of sinners against himself' [*Heb.* 12:3]! How patiently he corrects the errors of his own disciples! How affectionately he seeks them out in their lost state, calls them to himself in a variety of ways, comforts, teaches and prepares them for his departure and then prays to the Father for them [*John* 17] that they and all their number to come will triumph over every obstacle and arrive in glory at last! Indeed, he prays not only that they may arrive in the glory but, more than all abstract excellences, he prays as his last petition: 'that the love wherewith thou hast loved me may be in them and I in them' [*John* 17:26]. Our Saviour is not content that we should merely have heaven or love or glory. He wills that we should have *him*. For to a believer Christ is more than heaven and his presence better than crowns, thrones or diadems of splendour. Knowing this therefore, he carries the sublime tenor of his sacerdotal prayers to the very last syllable of our desire and swells our spiritual joy to its full diapason: 'I in them' [v.26].

'Tis mystery all—th' Immortal dies.' Well does Charles Wesley state the awesome wonder we must feel when we view the cross of Christ, or rather the One who dies on the cross. The apostle Paul speaks of the four dimensions of Christ's love, as love with 'length and breadth and depth and height' [*Eph.* 3:18]. The proof of our small grace is our small gratitude to Christ for this, the *magnum opus* of his love towards us. But love is in every action, every word, every passion and every pang upon the cross. Not till he has carried his mediatorial task to the uttermost point of our need does he allow himself to relax in the sleep of death. But by then the cry 'It is finished!' is echoing and reverberating in every atom of the universe, not only in the rending of the veil and opening up of the Holy of holies, not only in the cracking of the graves of Old Testament saints, but in the remotest corners of this sin-cursed universe, in which now there is to be heard a groaning and travailing in birth till a rejuvenated universe at last appears [*Rom.* 8:22, *2 Pet.* 3:10].

It must not be allowed to cross our thoughts that Christ's love has now all been exhausted because the exhibition of it on Calvary was so extravagant. The same pure and perfect pitch of love in Christ is beating in his soul towards every one of his saints as surely today as in the day of his bloody agony and self-offering. It is this wonderful love which makes him ardent with desire for the day of his espousals, when his Bride shall be brought to him. Much he has loved her and much he has yearned for her to be consummated in union with himself. Through all ages of the earth's history he has watched her progress on earth and seen her faithfulness to him, often expressed in martyrdom and tears. He has loved to hear her voice and delighted in her confidences. Just as for her 'to live is Christ', so for him, as Husband of his Bride, to live, die, rise and intercede has been the church. No two beings shall ever exist for one another so completely as do Christ and the church. As he has died to have her eternally with him, so she in this world has gone 'through fire and water' [*Ps.* 66:12], even through floods of torture and of blood for his sake. But the Church's torments and sufferings have only proved the truth of the inspired word, that 'many waters cannot quench love, neither can the floods drown it' [*Song of Sol.* 8:7], for 'love is strong as death; jealousy is cruel as the grave; the coals thereof are coals of fire, which hath a most vehement flame' [v.6]. Christ and the church belong together in the eternal counsels of God; they will be together in the eternal ages of the world to come.

Let the believer think much and often of the love of Christ. By all right means let him stir up his thoughts of this mysterious Lover of his soul. Christ is more than a Saviour. He is a Husband, flesh of our flesh and bone of our bone [*Eph.* 5:30]. It is a mistake to suppose that Christ has only repaired the harm done by Adam. He has done far more. Christ has done more for our good than Adam ever did for our hurt. He has raised us above angels to sit on his throne. He has lifted us to the highest level possible for created beings, that of eternal ingrafting into the God-Man. If Satan's lie 'ye shall be as gods' [*Gen.* 3:5] was the bait to drag us to hell, Christ's obedience and blood have been the means both to lift us out of sin and well-nigh to raise us, were that possible, to be as 'gods' indeed. Gods, certainly, we are not and shall never be. But the love of Christ has exalted us to as close a nearness to that as it is permissible or desirable in any creatures to be.

There are many blessings for the believer in frequently recalling the love of Christ. Not the least of these is the flood of joy which it brings to his heart. Joy is good for us. It unites all the faculties of the soul and generates fresh strength for service and for sacrifice. It may be a part of the answer we are looking for in these days to the problem of 'burn out' and 'break down' among Christian workers. So long as we look at the wind and weather of our temptations or discouragements we shall sink beneath the waves. But a fresh cordial of joy from the cup of Christ's salvation will do much to send us about his work rejoicing. In so saying, of course, we do not mean to speak unkindly of any Christian whose health has been broken through excess of labours. But we do believe that a 'felt Christ' is one great need of the hour to counteract our miseries.

If our heart remains cold after all we can do to conjure up in our minds the wonders of Christ's love towards us, we must be ruthless with our affections and constrain our slow hearts to measure our debt of thankfulness to Jesus by a consideration of the gulf between our blessings and our deservings. Let us recall with deepest mortification that if Christ is my life, I was his death. If he is my righteousness, I was his damnation. As he is all my blessing, I was once his curse, his scourge, his 'hell'. O what a contradiction of God I was when Christ found me and renewed the divine image upon my soul! O at what a distance from God I was when Jesus breathed life into me and bade me live in the near presence of his Father! So let every believer think and ponder often in his heart till the fire burns and the heart of stone melts in solemn appreciation of what we owe to him whose Name is above every name that ever shall be.

The believer whose heart feels the love of Christ will find he has at once a well-tuned harp with which to sing God's praises. He has a Guest who will 'sup' with him [*Rev.* 3:20], a Comforter who will visit him [*John* 14:18], a Friend who will treat him in this present life above the level of 'servants' and who delights to term us his 'friends' [*John* 15:15].

We began this chapter by suggesting that nothing is more surprising in all creation than the love of Christ. Perhaps we should add, however, the equally surpassing fact that so very few on earth appear to have any desire to know Christ's love. But even that makes electing grace the sweeter.

11

Our Unpopular Lord Jesus

The world has no great figure in all its long history who can at all compare with our blessed Lord Jesus Christ for unpopularity. Even rogues and demons incarnate have their earthly admirers and their determined supporters. But Jesus stands alone as having none to love him out of this dark world. If the believing reader is ready to jump up in protest and to declare *his* attachment to Christ, we shall meekly reply to him that he does not belong to this dark world and it is of those who do that we now speak.

The unpopularity of Jesus is as strange and remarkable as his very person. It is a feature of his ministry to which God draws careful attention even in the prophetic Scriptures. Isaiah speaks in these terms of the unpopularity of Jesus: 'To him whom man despiseth, to him whom the nation abhorreth, to a servant of rulers' [*Isa.* 49:7]. In a more familiar passage Isaiah refers to our unpopular Saviour in this way: 'he hath no form nor comeliness . . . there is no beauty that we should desire him. He is despised and rejected of men . . . we hid as it were our faces from him; he was despised and we esteemed him not' [*Isa.* 53:2-3].

There is an obvious reference in these words to the rejection of Christ by the Jews. John alludes to this when he informs us concerning Jesus Christ that 'he came unto his own, and his own received him not' [*John* 1:11]. But the reference does not begin or end there, for John has just finished informing us of the fact that Christ 'was in the *world*, and the *world* was made by him, and the *world* knew him not' [*John* 1:10]. So rejection of Jesus Christ is not exclusively a Jewish thing And rejection of Jesus is not to become the basis for anti-semitic sentiment as it has so often been unjustly made to be. The Jews are not the only nation to mistreat and reject the Lord Jesus Christ. The whole world has done so. It is mankind as a whole which 'abhors Christ' [*Isa.* 49:7]. The world's hatred of Jesus Christ is a remarkable phenomenon from any point of view but it is an indisputable fact. The passing of the years, admittedly, alters a little the precise form of this hatred. But it is always there and it is always fundamentally the same general attitude of enmity and disfavour.

In the days of the early church, men's low opinion of Christ expressed itself in a variety of curious ways. Some rejected his manhood, some his Godhood, others confused and confounded the relation between both his manhood and his Godhood. In the Middle Ages, Jesus Christ was ostensibly honoured by all the countries of Europe. But they hid the glory of Christ behind Mary, the papacy and the priesthood. When the Reformers came forward to champion Christ's honour they brought on themselves the wrath of half the world. The nineteenth-century Liberals found a Saviour who is 'very God of very God, begotten not created' a doctrine too hard to swallow. So they invented a 'Kenotic Christ' who left all his glory behind at birth.

Our own generation has excelled all others in its dislike of Jesus. Belief in any of the supernatural aspects of our Saviour's life and ministry is resented like poison, whether we think of his miraculous birth, his redemptive passion, his coming back from the grave or his claim to be the only way back to God.

It has been well said that those who have written a 'Life of

Christ' tell us much more about themselves than about him. Many authors of such 'Lives' have preferred not to see what they find in the four Gospels and have chosen rather to look down the deep well of their own critical surmisings. What they have seen has been their own Higher Critical faces which they have proceeded to paint for us as the 'authentic Jesus'. But the 'authentic Jesus' is seldom the same in any two such 'Lives'.

In the nineteenth-century 'Life' by the German scholar David Strauss (1808-74) we had a mythical Christ. In the 'Life' by Ernest Renan (1823-92) we had an amiable Galilean preacher. The Christ of F. W. Farrar's (1831-1903) 'Life' is one suited to the Victorian middle-class in England, to whom the idea of propitiation was becoming repugnant. Albert Schweitzer (1875-1965) offered us, in his book *The Quest for the Historical Jesus* (1910), a Christ who mistakenly expected a speedy end to this world and, when he discovered he was wrong, concluded he needed to suffer to save his people from the tribulation of the last days. The Jesus of Adolph Harnack (1851-1930) was the living embodiment of love and idealism. For Karl Barth (1886-1968), with his theology of paradox, Jesus is the 'Yes' and the 'No' of God. Paul Tillich (1886-1965) presents us with a Jesus who is no more than a symbol. And so on, till today our religious spokesmen are happy just to present us with a Jesus who had something or other to do with 'the myth of God incarnate'.

The unpopularity of Jesus, reflected in these and a myriad other attempts to re-write his life and ministry, is not something which arises out of a rational dislike for some abnormality in his character. If it did it might be partly excusable. But, on the contrary, enmity to the meek and lowly Saviour of men arises out of a thorough dislike of his purity and perfection. Admittedly, there is more to it than that. Scholars have fallen over one another to take issue with his claims to uniqueness, his miracles, his power to forgive sin, his foreknowledge of coming events and such things. But what most hurts the secular mind about Christ is his 'otherness'. He is different from any other who ever lived. He cannot be bracketed along with others. He fits no categories. He is special and he is good. These are what men love least in others.

The hatred which men feel for Christ, in a word, is just that very thing which he himself foresaw and foretold through the psalmist: 'They that hate me without a cause are more than the hairs of mine head' [Ps. 69:4]. As the haters are innumerable, so the cause of their hatred is non-existent. But if the hatred of the world towards Christ is without a cause, it can only be one thing—malignity, which means unprovoked spite and ill. The world loathes our Jesus just because he is all that he is: holy, perfect, loving, patient, divine and Godlike in person and in action.

The world hates Jesus Christ more than anyone else who ever lived on earth. The popularity rating of our holy Saviour is at the lowest possible point in the eyes of mankind. They would be happier to let Barabbas, and a whole world of Barabbases, go free rather than leave Jesus alone when they had it in their power to hurt him. Where a Jesus is at hand to be hated, a Herod and a Pilate will be ready to patch up old quarrels. A great hatred drives out all lesser ones. Anything is preferable to the godless than Someone in whose holy face shines all the glory of God and in whose pure eyes is visible all the holiness of heaven itself.

It was a foolish as well as a cruel thing in the Middle Ages for 'Christians' to spurn the Jews for their crucifixion of our Lord Jesus Christ. The folly lay in men not seeing that when the Jews put him to death by the hand of the Roman authorities, they were not acting for Jews alone but for *all* mankind. The crime of the Jews was immensely great and they have suffered immensely for it over the centuries. But our attitude should be that of sorrow and pity for them as we realize that of the Gentiles, too, it could and can be said: 'We hid as it were our faces from him; he was despised and we esteemed him not' [*Isa.* 53:3]. Jew and Gentile stand together in this sense. Our essential attitude to the glorious Lord from heaven is the same in every respect: 'We will not have this man to reign over us' [*Luke* 19:14].

This is what is so vexatious about Jesus Christ. It is the authority of his mind and word which we intuitively recognize to be absolute and divine. It at once inspires resentment in us if we do not belong to him through faith. The devils recognized it and cried out in fear. The Pharisees and chief priests sensed it and they could not rest till they had him nailed to the cross. The heretics feel it and they are prepared to twist any text of Scripture like a nose of wax to cut Christ down to manageable proportions. The critics are aware of it and they cower when the shadow of this awesome Jesus falls across them. But till their eyes are opened by faith they will go on with their age-old mischief of cutting the Jesus of the Gospels down to a size they can cope with. They grace their science with the title of 'scholarship'; in reality it is nothing but hatred of Christ's authority and Godhead.

Who can deny that this fallen world is a madhouse, when one considers this attitude of abhorrence on the part of mankind towards the Lord Jesus Christ? Sin has made us all mad as well as bad. For we are so stupefied and besotted with our love of sin that we fail, till we are converted, to see that Christ is the only true friend we sinners have.

To run away from Jesus is to turn away from the fountain of all grace and love. To be religious but not to crown Christ as Lord of all is to insult God and injure ourselves eternally. To 'taste' something of the sweet joys of the gospel and to refuse to bend the knee to Jesus is tantamount to grieving the Spirit of God and crucifying Christ afresh to ourselves [*Heb.* 6:4-6]. It is to commit apostasy and to place ourselves where it is 'impossible' to be 'renewed unto repentance' [*Heb.* 6:4]. To what then shall we liken the Higher Critics and the liberal theologians who have placed Christ on their Procrustean bed and lopped off his Godhead, glory and grace? They are like children playing with their father's car on a rainy day and who put on the windscreen wipers and say, 'See, we have stopped the rain!' but, unfortunately for those who find fault with a faultless Christ and who stumble over the stumblingstone of a Man who is also the incarnate God, Jesus is not in the smallest degree diminished by their low opinions of him. He remains the Lord of glory still, after all that the demythologizers have done to cork Christ down firmly into their critical bottle.

Worse still—and the news is very bad indeed—this same Jesus shall come again one day in all the glory which his Father has conferred upon him for his faithfully finished work for fallen sinners. Ah, with what eyes will men then look into the eyes of Jesus when they have spent a lifetime denying him! What a choking of voices there is yet to be in the throats of all who have spoken against the Jesus of the Bible, when they are called on in the Last Day to confess him 'Lord of all'! And when the Jesus we have spoken of opens his mouth to pronounce his final sentence upon the wicked, what ghastly, frightened suspense will grip the hearts of all Christ-hating men!

It has yet to be made manifest whether the Christ-denying Higher Critic will be more favourably placed in that day than ordinary, common sinners, or whether his doom will be still less tolerable than that of others who knew the Bible little. As for us, we would much prefer to love and serve this blessed yet unpopular Saviour with our every breath until we see him in a better world and there find grace to praise him in a way worthy of his glorious divinity. Everyone who loves the Lord will say, Amen!

III

The Christian's Walk

See then that ye walk circumspectly,
not as fools, but as wise.

Ephesians 5:15.

12

At Home in the Heavenlies

The act of God in our regeneration is so momentous that no single category of thought is sufficient to describe the changes it brings about in and for us. It is an eruption from death to life, a translation from darkness to light, an initiation from folly into wisdom, a second birth and begetting, a transition from a broken covenant to a saving covenant, a manumission from thraldom and tyranny into glorious freedom, an immigration from the land of nonentity into full citizenship—in a word, a coming home to God.

So vast are the implications, indeed, of the act of regeneration that Paul, to draw our languid attention to what God has done in us, uses a phrase which all but defies our analysis and comprehension. He announces that we are 'in the heavenlies'. This phrase occurs only five times in his writings and is to be found only in the Epistle to the Ephesians. The term cannot merely mean 'in heavenly things' because, as Charles Hodge points out, it almost always has a local sense. In more than one occurrence of the phrase there is the idea of a dynamic divine exaltation from a lower to a higher sphere or realm [*Eph.* 1:20; 2:6] . In our familiarity with the *words* we are apt to overlook the remarkable fact that the same location in the heavenly sphere is attributed to believers as is attributed to Christ himself. And it is attributed to us *now* and not simply beyond the veil of time.

It is not easy for our minds to appreciate that we are already in heavenly places. We are accustomed to thinking of heaven as a place and a state still future. Certainly we are not in heaven yet. There is the intermediate state of heaven after death. Better still, there is a full and complete state of heaven after the judgement, where we shall be made perfect in body and soul with the Lord forever. Heaven is still future. But the heavenly state is present to God's people in at least one sense; and this is what we find difficult to define. However, Paul has placed it on record that already God 'hath raised us up together, and made us sit together in heavenly places in Christ Jesus' [*Eph.* 2:6].

It is tempting to define our sitting in Christ in the heavenlies in terms of nothing more than a representative sense. Christ is there literally; we are there representatively. This interpretation of the phrase yields good doctrine, certainly. He is there as our Head and, as such, he guarantees our future presence in heaven since we are the members of his mystical body. But there is good reason to believe that this insight, precious as it is, does not exhaust the apostle's thought when he declares that believers are now seated in the heavenlies in Christ Jesus.

In addition to the thought of Christ's representation of his people in heaven is the idea of their present spiritual union with him. The life which flows in us is a heavenly life. The sap, so to speak, which nourishes the souls of God's saints on earth is of a heavenly source and origin. Even while we are still here on earth we partake of a celestial energy, which is being daily and even hourly imparted to our hearts by Christ. The life of God's saints is even now furnished and fed out of that same crystal fountain which they are all to drink from eternally in their final resting place. It is a life which is 'hid with Christ in God' [*Col.* 3:3], to us and to the world invisible and secret, yet real and supernatural.

But there is surely more still implied even than this in the apostle's declaration that we are seated in the heavenlies. The term is so brilliantly felicitous that it could only come by supernatural inspiration. As a phrase divinely chosen, it conveys the impression of state and even of status through the imagery of geographical location. To be seated in an aerial position is to be above all the world. It is to enjoy a privileged vantage-point, from which we see and know what others cannot see or know.

This is exactly what the people of God now enjoy. They are in a state of grace and that is a state in which they are enabled to see the vanity of all earthly power and glory and the transience of all that is done 'under the sun'. To be in the heavenlies is to be in the very suburbs of glory. We do not yet see the sights that we shall see hereafter. But we are already aware of them. Like villagers who have travelled from the countryside towards a great capital city and become aware of the distant hubbub of the city while they are still on its outskirts, and before they reach the city gates, so believers are already conscious of the stir within the celestial city into which they have not yet quite entered. Through our acquaintance with God and his Word we are in a degree familiar already with the secret agencies of providence, with spiritual interventions, with divine decrees, the sounding of trumpets, the emptying of vials, the ascending and descending of angels, the song of the redeemed, the opening of the seals, the cries of souls under the altar, the thunderings of Sinai and, above all, the mediation of the Son of God between earth and heaven. These things are the constant commerce of heaven and those who live in the suburbs of the city become accustomed to the distant sound of them because of their relative proximity.

Older theologians used to explain 'the heavenlies' in the following way. The visible heavens (or sky) they termed the heaven of nature (*caelum naturae*); the place of bliss where God is visible they called the heaven of glory (*caelum gloriae*); the 'heavenly places' of the Epistle to the Ephesians they termed the heaven of grace (*caelum gratiae*). The distinction is excellent. That is just the term we are searching for. Believers are already in the heaven of grace. 'Grace is young glory,' as our Puritan forefathers aptly put it. Grace is glory in the bud; and glory will be grace in full flower. The two are not absolutely separate states. The one is preparatory to the other and leads into it by an inevitable progression .

This is not true of the two states which precede the state of grace. The state of innocence in which Adam was created could not be said to be the natural precursor of the state of either sin or confirmed holiness. It was a probationary state, mutable and unstable as yet. Similarly, the state of sin into which Adam's fall brought the whole human race was not a natural precursor of the state of grace. On the contrary, it was the preliminary phase of everlasting death. But the state of grace most emphatically *is* a preliminary, and a foretaste even, of glory, immortality and eternal life in heaven.

The point we need to see is that the state of grace is nearer to the state of glory than it is to the state of sin. Believers are nearer in character to God and the angels than they are to unregenerate and lost sinners. The good that they will is greater than the evil which they do. This is so because grace in believers is more truly their character than indwelling sin.

There is no continuity between the states of sin and of grace. But there is great continuity between grace and glory. If God has delivered us from sin to grace, much more will he translate us from grace to glory. There is more divine intervention required to lift us from sin to grace than from grace to glory. This appears to be implied in what Paul states in Romans 5:9-10. That we are now regenerate argues that we must shortly be perfect. God has lifted us from the grave of sin and he will shortly lift us from the grave of death also.

It remains to state, in conclusion, that we must strive to cultivate daily a demeanour and a bearing of heart and mind which are consistent with our heavenly position in Christ. Of Richard Sibbes it was said that 'heaven was in him before he was in heaven'. This is true in a measure of all the regenerate. But the great Christians of the past and their writings are supremely valuable because they share with us the secret of a consistent spirituality. They were in heaven as to their affections long before their souls got there. May we too learn to be at home in the heavenlies!

13

A Time to Afflict the Soul

There is a time when the believer becomes aware that he is spiritually dead. The deadness we speak of is not, of course, that spiritual death which is the condition of every man without Christ. The unbeliever's deadness is total. He is a corpse in a spiritual grave. All that the unbeliever does in the way of religious activity has the smell of death upon it. Unregenerate prayer, unregenerate worship, unregenerate service is valueless to a holy God. It cannot please him but rather is detestable in his sight.

The deadness which periodically afflicts the believer is never total but always partial. It is, however, a serious disease of the soul and weakens him in every way. He prays still; but his prayers are languid and formal. He goes through the motions of all spiritual duty; but he is uneasily aware that all is not well with himself. He feels like a man in a dream or in a daze. A film of worldliness has somehow coated over every faculty of his heart and mind. He tries to shake off his lethargy but finds it alarmingly difficult to do so. He no longer lives consciously upon the life that is in Christ but goes through the routine of service to God more because he ought to do it than because he wants to.

There is not one Christian in a thousand who would deny that this experience of deadness comes upon him at times. It is but too frequent and too common. It is the condition reflected in the words, 'I sleep, but my heart waketh' [*Song of Sol.* 5:2]. This is the state of soul which we must take notice of in ourselves.

One lesson we may learn from it is that our souls, being clogged with corruption, are constantly deceiving us into a state of formalism and hypocrisy. One day we seek Christ with all our hearts and find him. But then we imperceptibly decline in earnestness. We cease to pant after God. We do not pursue him till we find him and get his felt presence. Next we grow accustomed to living at a distance from him. When months, perhaps, have gone by we become guiltily conscious that something has gone wrong with our relationship with God. The dew is not on our spirits. The sun of righteousness does not shine upon our hearts. A damp mist or fog has covered the landscape of the soul and God is enjoyed only in theory but not as a present reality. All this is a sure sign that we have unwittingly drifted into formalism. We have lost our ardour and are following afar off.

Another lesson we are to learn from our periodic deadness is that the Lord Jesus Christ will hide himself from us when we do not genuinely desire him. It is a moot point as to whether Christ ever withdraws from his people without provocation. But there can be no doubt that when we cease to value his communion and fellowship he may withdraw his felt presence from us. When he detects within us that careless attitude which leaves us indifferent to his love and grace, he commonly absents himself from us for a time until we realize what we have done and so run after him again with tears, crying, 'Saw ye him whom my soul loveth?' [*Song of Sol.* 3:3]

A time of spiritual death is not a thing to be taken lightly by us as Christians. When the soul sleeps the owls of the night fly abroad. Temptations flit across the believer's life with sevenfold mischief. It is the harvest time of the devil when we follow Christ from afar. Now Satan sees the hour he has long waited for in which we sleep on the lap of carelessness. He will strike when the iron is hot. He will, if he can, approach us at that hour with the shears to cut off our locks of consecration and render us a blow which we may never recover from all our life.

There is, seemingly, a sort of praying even by hell and by Satan [*Job* 1-2]. Awesome as it is and steeped in deep mystery, even hell has its desires and its requests, of which God is informed. What else can this mean but that Satan pleads against God's people in this life that he might do them some injury and spite? If the doctrine appears novel we must call to mind Christ's fearful words: 'Simon, Simon, behold, Satan hath *desired* to have you, that he may sift you as wheat' [*Luke* 22:31]

We cannot afford to be ignorant of Satan's 'desires', of which our merciful Intercessor here speaks. Even when informed of his danger, Peter did not heed his warning and it took a bitter personal fall to bring him to see the reality of what our Lord had graciously forewarned him about. Christ's intercession guaranteed that Peter would not fall away. But it did not go the length of preventing Peter's fall. The fault was not in any weakness in Christ's intercessory ministry. Our Lord may leave us to be badly scratched and mauled by the roaring lion on occasions, especially when we are too carnally confident to heed his advice.

We do not always recover from the consequences of a bad fall. Even when we do we may go all our lives in sorrow that we brought reproach on ourselves or even on the cause of God by our carelessness. If we are to get cleanly through without a blot we shall need to walk closely with Christ and we cannot afford ever to neglect his call to 'keep the heart with all diligence' [*Prov.* 4:23].

When we feel deadness of heart (and assuming the cause is not physical exhaustion), we are to look for the remedy only by repentance. Repentance ought to be a believer's daily and hourly companion. Brokenness of heart and tenderness of spirit should be the hallmark of our whole character. Every emotion we have needs to be sweetened and purged with this spirit of penitence. But, though this is true as a general rule of life, there is a place for special repentance in our experience when we find ourselves spiritually dead. It is in repentance that our deliverance lies.

We make no spiritual progress apart from repentance. When we come to our Bibles and to good books, or else to prayer and preaching it will be found true that we get good and feel God's blessing in proportion as we handle these means of grace with tenderness of heart and with self-abasement. It is not the having of spiritual privileges which yields the advantage or confers the blessing upon us. It is the having of a humble heart and an exercised spirit as we handle the things of God. This accounts to a large extent for the experience we all have, that some days we learn a great deal from our books and other days we learn next to nothing from them. Some days we are aware of a cup which is full and running over, while on other days we feel as if we were in a dry, parched land. If we search out the cause of this difference it will be found to have a great deal to do with the measure of our repenting.

It is only the Antinomian who thinks that the Christian has no need to go on repenting. The truly biblical attitude is that which Tertullian long ago expressed in the words: 'I was born for nothing but repentance.' The pity is that we today are almost all Antinomians. Repentance in secret is rather read about admiringly in old biographies than actually practised in the life. But how different were great saints of better days! Look at the iron rod with which a Calvin ruled his own spirit! Look at the rigorous fastings of the Puritans! Look at the spiritual mortifications of a Brainerd or a M'Cheyne. Or listen to the anguished ejaculations of a Jonathan Edwards as he audibly lamented and bewailed his sins in the ear of God as he walked alone among the woods of New England.

If repentance is unpopular among modern Christians it can only be because we have a false view of sin and therefore have an urgent need to study the theme of sin again in biblical light. Sin is arguably the greatest power in existence but for the power of God himself. It is not only an evil but an infinite evil. It is a universal evil. Sin is not only wrong but totally wrong. It is not merely against God but absolutely and entirely against God. Sin is the contradiction of God and the antithesis of his nature. If its origin is a mystery so, too, to a great extent is its subtlety and craft. Sin is contempt for God, disregard for law, imperious self-ishness and defiance of all that is good or right. Left to run its course unchecked sin would ravage the whole universe and even assault the throne of God with impunity. It knows no shame. It cares for no consequences. It heeds no bounds.

The Antinomian response to sin is to say that there is always grace in God. This is the same as saying that when we sin we need have no fear because there is always mercy. Christ is not given to us to enable us to sin without fear or shame. That would be to make Christ the minister of sin. It belongs to the subtlety of sin that it tells religious persons there is always a Christ to go to. But the grace of God which is in a real Christian will not allow him to be at rest in sin. A believer who has sinned is like a man who is required to be his own executioner. He expostu-lates with himself and loathes himself. He applies, of course, to Christ for grace and pardon but is never at his ease till the Spirit of God heals his smart and pours oil on his wounds. This the Antinomian does for himself. But the exercised Christian waits on God with salt tears of repentance and walks softly till the fire of his guilt is extinguished in his conscience.

If sin were the trifling thing many today in churches think it to be, why should Christ have counselled us to be so ruthless in resisting it? Why should a man need to 'pluck out his right eye' or 'cut off his right hand' [*Matt.* 5:29-30] if sin in the believer were a matter of only minor importance? And if sin poses no serious threat to the man of God, why should an apostle require to buffet his body and keep it in subjection [*1 Cor.* 9:27]? The fact is that sin is sin in the Christian and its power in the Christian is fearfully strong. If it is not strong enough to ruin us eternally, it is no thanks to sin but only to Christ who undertook to lead all believers at last to glory. But sin can wreak havoc in the life of any believer if not watched against. Experience should have taught us all this. Similarly, it can wreak havoc in a believer's family and in the church.

There is only one attitude possible for us if we mean to get to heaven. We must wage a ceaseless warfare against sin within us all the days of our life. Therefore, whenever we are overtaken in a fault or whenever we find that our souls have fallen fast asleep, we had better resort to violent measures to extricate ourselves before a greater mischief befalls us. By this advice, we mean that we must then afflict our souls before God and plead in earnest to be aroused from slumber.

Everything in this modern world is somehow inexplicably geared to inducing sleep in our souls. Modern society is a verit-able cave of Morpheus—the mythological place where men forgot reality and succumbed to dreams. This is one reason why the modern Christian must keep up his spiritual and theological reading. We need to read for dear life. It is imperative that we do not fall asleep with the whole of the rest of society round about us. Nothing matters to those who sleep in Morpheus' cave today except plays, programmes and sporting fixtures. It is not easy to resist the spirit of the age. But one essential way is to keep up our reading especially of the great writers of the past. For instance, when we have settled on our lees and are on good terms with ourselves, let us go to the biography of John Duncan, the learned Hebrew Professor of the Free Church of Scotland a century and a half ago. He will prove healthful medicine for a mood of complacency.

Few men have detested easy arm-chair Christianity as much as 'Rabbi' Duncan did. He feared it like the plague in case he should become shallow and spiritually unfeeling. Let one passage of his *Life* suffice.[1]

> The 'gentle conviction of sin, the calm, coldish admiration of Christ, the gentlemanly, scholarlike, prudent gratitude, the obedience of a freezing but not absolutely frozen state', he detested in others as well as dreaded in himself; and there was nothing into which he more earnestly entered, than any preaching or line of procedure that would help to break up such a condition of the Christian church. At all costs he would have it broken up in himself; and he did not care what offence of the cross might arise, what foolishness of preaching, what contempt of the worldly wise, or what displeasure of the religious world might ensue, if there might by any means be a shaking of this stagnation in the Christian community.

This attitude of Duncan towards sin and sleep of soul is the key to his profound spirituality and usefulness. He was undeniably eccentric and unquestionably brilliant. But what matters most is that he was a very conscientious and devout believer. To this day his name is a household word in many places of the Highlands. If any today fail to see his greatness as a Christian it may put us on our guard to see how very little profound spirituality we have ever previously met. In short, it may serve to show us that we are—perhaps almost all of us—half asleep in religious complacency and shallowness.

If society is to be awakened one day from its deep slumber, it will only be done by Christians who have first woken up themselves to the full splendour of their privilege and who have taken seriously the call to live wholly and entirely for God. Such were the early Methodist preachers. Such was C. H. Spurgeon. They were men fully alive and fully awake in a world where others were either half asleep or fully drugged.

The earnest believer has taken note of these things. He weeps to see the whole world so easy in its sin. He yearns to see society roused and awakened to eternal gospel truths. Consequently he chastens his soul before God as a necessary part of his regular service to Christ. His motive is to call down upon himself and upon the whole church those powers of heaven by which the lost sons of men may be awakened. Daniel so afflicted his soul in his own day. So did Ezra and so did also Nehemiah. They made mortification and repentance principal duties of their otherwise very busy and active lives. And they did not wait on God in vain.

It is not in vain for us to afflict our souls before God for grace to help us in the present task. There is a golden hammer in the hand of God for breaking in pieces every mountain, and he must be earnestly sought by his people till he raises up a man who can wield that hammer of gold. A slothful, unfeeling religion is not the faith we read of in the Bible. There is such a thing as following the Lord *fully*. There is such a thing as fearing the Lord *greatly*. There is such a thing as the wish to see God glorified here and now *on earth*. Then let all right-hearted men pray for grace to cast off the mantle of complacency and gird up their loins with fresh zeal for the task.

14

The Management of Our Pride

It is a curious fact of experience that every man must boast about something. The man who boasts of nothing at all is a being unknown and unheard of in this world. The mind of man, so it would appear, is hinged in so marvellous a manner that, were he still holy and unfallen, his thoughts would be for ever constantly flowing out of himself to God in an ecstasy of praise and delight. Sin has not altered this constitutional tendency of his soul; but it has directed the soul to different objects, so that, instead of turning to God his Maker, he now turns with perverse delight to adore the creature.

There are, in the nature of things, only two ultimate objects to which a man's soul may incline with proud pleasure. He may turn to God or else to himself.

MAN'S BONDAGE

The Christless man is in the unenviable position of being a slave to himself. It is not simply that he *is* so but that he cannot help being so. 'Ye shall be as gods' [*Gen.* 3:5] was the tempter's whisper to our first parents, and it was fulfilled when man fell, but in a manner which was hideous and fiendish. There occurred in the faculties of man's soul at the Fall a revolution and a realignment of affection which was to have catastrophic consequences.

Whereas before it was instinctive for man to boast in God, from now on it became instinctive for him to boast in himself. Man, by the Fall, was smitten with a Narcissus complex. By some mysterious judgement of God, the chemistry of the soul was altered by this first entrance of sin. The orientation of every human faculty was introverted. It turned in upon itself. God was exiled to the periphery and self was set up high on the throne of man's mind. To reverse this tragic slavery to self and so to break the adamantine chains that bind us to our natural love of vainglory requires infinite power.

THE NEW BIRTH

It is this which occurs at the new birth. This is what the new birth is. It is nothing less than a gracious forth-putting of God's infinite energy within the chaos of man's fallen faculties in order to realign them, in principle, to what they were before the Fall. The new birth precedes faith in us. To suggest, as too many have done, that we must believe in order to be born again is as absurd as to say that the bulb must shine before the light-switch can be turned on. Faith in man is not the energy which produces the new birth nor is it the condition which God requires in order to perform his work of power.

On the contrary, faith is the evidence that the new birth has occurred already in man's soul. In that sense, it is 'not of yourselves: it is the gift of God' [*Eph.* 2:8]. Faith is impossible before God makes the soul live, because faith is an activity of a soul made alive. Faith, like all the other evangelical graces, is the fruit of the Spirit's prior action in man. To define faith as an action possible to the unsaved sinner is to dignify man's fallen will with omnipotence and at the same time to offer an insult to God our Saviour. This is the theory of our new birth. It is elementary to the properly taught Christian. But not so elementary or easy to

109

him is the practical outworking of the doctrine. It is to this that we now turn.

PRACTICAL EFFECT

It must follow from what we have stated that the characteristic behaviour of true Christianity is to give all the glory to God. If the Fall so disarranged the faculties of our mind that we gloried as sinners in ourselves, it must follow that the new birth has rearranged our faculties so that we glory as Christians in God alone. This we should do and actually do when we act according to that which is most characteristic of us as God's children. For in our deepest desire we cannot but make our boast of him. We do not glorify him *perfectly*, it is true, but we do so heartily and sincerely.

No Christian, however, travels far on the pilgrim road before he experiences a disconcerting impulse within his nature to boast in himself. Two emotions follow hard on the heels of this guilty exaltation of self. The first is one of pleasure; every man loves his own praise. Self-love is sweet as honey to us; at least, it is for a brief moment. The second emotion, however, is one of shame that we have allowed ourselves to act, or even to think, so completely out of character. For self-love is idolatry in the soul.

WHEN WE BOAST

When the Christian glories in himself, he is usually soon made aware of his guilt. A shadow crosses his mind and the light of God's countenance is withdrawn. He becomes troubled in conscience. The Christian who is lifted up with proud thoughts of self-love is made to feel awkward, unclothed and naked before the bar of God's judgement. The veil of his peace is then forcibly stripped off from him.

When conscience has done its faithful work, there follow further reactions of the soul—self-loathing and self-scrutiny.

With bated breath the believer takes stock of his heinous crime. God, who is loved and acknowledged to be supremely lovable, is now reckoned to have been robbed of his rightful honour. To the spiritual mind, this robbery is counted as treason. Rightly and justly the soul now turns to become its own accuser and reproaches itself in the sternest terms: 'Oh rascal, proud heart within me, thou hast robbed God! Oh my soul, thou hast played the part of Satan who sought to raise himself above God's throne! Thou fool, my heart, fall into the dust and beg God's pardon, in case he be wounded and grieved with this devilry!'

The art of being a Christian is very largely the art of managing the corruptions of our soul. It is such a daunting task that God, who alone knows what is in man, describes it as a more difficult and skilful labour than that of statesmen or military generals: 'He that is slow to anger is better than the mighty: and he that ruleth his spirit than he that taketh a city' [*Prov.* 16:32].

To capture a town in war and to tyrannize over it when captured are tasks possible to men without supernatural strength. But only divine grace can enable man to govern his own spirit and to mortify his instinctive love of human praise. The best Christian is the one who best manages his soul and most ruthlessly strikes the serpent of pride with the sword of mortification. No pride ever appears in the New Testament portrait of Christ.

THE LIBERAL 'JESUS'

The liberal view of Jesus is a logical absurdity because it tries to have its cake and eat it. The liberal theology wants to have a human Jesus and at the same time a Jesus whom we can admire. But this is a hopeless task. If the Jesus of the Gospels is only human, then there has never lived a greater megalomaniac. What admiration is owed to a mere man who can claim: 'I and my Father are one' [*John* 10:30] or 'Before Abraham was, I am' [*John* 8:58]? If

Jesus is only what Modernists have made of him, then his claims are fully as blasphemous as the Jews of his day regarded them. There is only one conclusion to be drawn from the liberal concept of Jesus and it is that we cannot possibly admire him or entertain his claims.

No theological view of Jesus fits his claims but the apostolic one, that he is the incarnate God, who may command the absolute obedience of all mankind forever. But liberal theology has in the last hundred years emptied the churches more effectively than a horde of Saracens could have done, because it made him a mere man. It was not long before the man-in-the-street realized that a mere man does not have a right to our *worship* and so he left the pew years ago. Liberal theology has changed its name but today it still reigns in many pulpits and continues to deny the glory of Christ.

The real Christ is (marvellous to relate!) the meekest man who ever lived. Considering that he is the Lord of glory, he showed on earth a meekness under every form of ill-treatment which mystified even the brutal Pilate. No man ever governed his own human spirit as did the Lord Jesus Christ. Though scrutinized daily by a thousand enemies, he never betrayed, even momentarily, the faintest trace of selfishness, impatience or unjustifiable anger.

OUR NEED FOR LIKENESS TO CHRIST
Pride is one of the commonest sins in the modern church and it proves how little we really know of 'the mind that was in Christ Jesus' [*Phil.* 2:5]. One man glories in gifts, another in numbers and a third in eloquence. As a generation of Christians we have little ability to manage our pride. To append the label 'Reformed' to our party will not suffice to cure this evil. It is greatly to be feared that we do not take seriously the call to 'humble ourselves

under the mighty hand of God' [*1 Pet.* 5:6] .

Happy is that believer who has learned to 'glory only in the cross of Christ' [*Gal.* 6:14]! Happy that church where boasting is abhorred and shunned! Man must boast of something. The world boasts of itself. This is what no Christian must ever allow himself to do. Do we want 'unction'? Do we want 'power'? Do we want 'revival'? It would be a major step towards all three if we could only learn to crucify our accursed pride more ruthlessly. For then we would experience God himself drawing nearer to us in our weakness. And what weakness we are in!

15

Redeeming the Tongue

When the Christian comes to the end of his pilgrimage, one sin he will regret is his idle speech. It is assumed that no true believer allows himself to go on in outward sins such as drunkenness, theft or immorality. It is assumed, too, that the believer is concerned to put a stop to all inward sins, not least to sinful thoughts. But there is reason to believe that our sins of speech are specially in need of correction.

Our sins of thought bring us much shame inwardly; but our sins of speech expose us to shame in the eyes of others. Our sinful words are our sinful thoughts verbalized. They are audibly broadcast. They reflect the corruption within us as in a mirror. They do harm to ourselves and they do harm to others.

Every Christian is profoundly thankful that many of his thoughts are known to no one besides himself and God. If the brain had a natural power of transmitting our private thoughts to other people, we should all be covered with confusion and disgrace. Who could look his neighbour in the eye? In kindness, however, God has erected a screen of privacy around the mind so that only he and we are aware of the constant trickle of unholy and foolish thoughts within us. Into this confessional, happily, no third party need be introduced.

But when our thoughts are clothed with speech, they remove

this screen of silence and pass through into the outside world. Our folly, formerly known only to ourselves, is now apparent to all men. It is to be feared, therefore, that we do not read God's Word on this subject with anything like the attention it deserves. 'The heart of fools proclaimeth foolishness' [*Prov.* 12:23]. 'The mouth of fools poureth out foolishness' [*Prov.* 15:2]. 'A foolish woman is clamorous [loud, noisy]' [*Prov.* 9:13]. 'A fool's lips enter into contention' [*Prov.* 18:6]. 'A fool's mouth is his destruction, and his lips are the snare of his soul' [*Prov.* 18:7]. 'A fool uttereth all his mind' [*Prov.* 29:11]. What shame a good man feels when he spoils his testimony by speaking foolishly! Scripture says: 'Dead flies cause the ointment of the apothecary [perfumer] to send forth a stinking savour: so doth a little folly him that is in reputation for wisdom and honour' [*Eccles.* 10:1].

HOLINESS

There is another reason, too, why we might look back in sorrow at our misuse of the tongue and therefore keep a more careful watch over it in the future. The tone of a Christian's conversation gives us a fair idea of how sanctified he is. 'By thy words thou shalt be justified, and by thy words thou shalt be condemned' [*Matt.* 12:37], said Christ. The meaning must surely be that words betray the true character of every man. They reveal the state of the heart and proclaim us worthy of heaven or hell. But if words reveal the state of the heart, do they not also reveal the degree of a Christian's holiness?

There is a wide difference between the everyday conversation of one Christian and another. All believers speak the language of heaven; but not all speak it equally consistently or fluently. If proof of this is required, we need only make the experiment of visiting half a dozen homes of Christian friends and neighbours. Every believer knows how little profit he gets from visiting some homes of professing Christians and, on the other hand, how much he gets from others. And it is not always as one might think. There are preachers whose table-talk is unprofitable, just as there are widows and orphans whose conversation is spiritual, holy and uplifting. Here sometimes, as elsewhere, 'the first are last and the last first'.

It must be owing to our ignorance of God that we sometimes permit our tongues to roam up and down in idle talk. Was it not our Saviour and Judge himself who warned us: 'I say unto you, That every idle word that men shall speak, they shall give account thereof in the day of judgment' [*Matt.* 12:36]? Similarly, the apostle Paul issues this sober command to us: 'Let no corrupt [worthless] communication proceed out of your mouth, but that which is good to the use of edifying, that it may minister grace unto the hearers' [*Eph.* 4:29]. There is a twofold duty placed before us in these words: to refrain from careless and unprofitable talk and to study to build one another up by well-chosen, soul-fattening conversation .

One reason why, as modern Christians, we talk so much about so little is that we are bombarded by trivial speech on every side. The entertainment world, which now has a mouth-piece somewhere in most houses, has a great deal to answer for. It has taught us all how to talk endlessly about nothing. So-called radio and television 'personalities' are often little better than mass educators in the art of trivial talk. That is the world's way and it is to be, in a sense, expected from them. But this bad example is picked up by Christians too. We learn to conform to ever easier and lower levels. Instead, we should raise the tone of our daily conversation to something more consistent with our calling as the sons of God.

How perfect in this respect, as in all others, is the example of our blessed Lord Jesus Christ! Let any atheist who cares to do so come forward with critical scissors and cut out from the four Gospels every saying of Christ's which is frothy, light and trivial. He will find it a hopeless task. Wherever we look in the Gospels, no single sermon, phrase or even syllable appears in the mouth of Jesus which could be called unprofitable. What a wealth, rather, we have of weighty doctrine from his lips! What an encyclopaedia of theology! What a compendium of holy living! What a 'book of quotations'! What an anthology of edifying and immortal sayings, stories, parables, prophecies and (even in our modern secular world) household expressions! If character is to be judged from a man's words, then we have here another reason for falling down at the feet of this Man, who so spoke as none ever did before or since. For Christ out-speaks all who ever spoke and makes the skill of an Aristotle grow pale. He out-Homers Homer and out-Shakespeares Shakespeare! One public sermon of Christ virtually makes the wisdom of the ages redundant; and his briefer words uttered in private carry the same hallmark of divine spirituality.

It is to be feared that our Saviour has too few disciples who study to copy him in his high-toned level of conversation. But, however greatly we have failed, we must repent and cultivate a way of speaking which better reflects the holiness of our Master.

PRACTICAL GUIDELINES

We would suggest the following guidelines as being a way to improve the tone of Christian conversation:

1. *When the Lord's people meet, they should always try to lead one another's thoughts to God.* Granted that we need to enquire after one another's families, health and circumstances, it should be our aim soon to rise in our talk to the things of the Spirit. We may do this by cultivating the habit of bringing the Scriptures into our con-

versation as a matter of course. It is surely a great pity if the heirs of heaven cannot talk naturally to one another about their Saviour and his Word. But as J. C. Ryle somewhere says, there are too many believers who 'in conference add nothing' to us [*Gal.* 2:6].

2.   *The Lord's people should attempt to cultivate a theological habit of mind and speech.* It is still the excellent practice of Christians in parts of the Highlands of Scotland to gather regularly in homes in order to spend two or three hours discussing points of Christian doctrine and experience. One wishes that the practice could be exported to every corner of the evangelical world. Over a period of years Christians become in this way familiar with the whole spectrum of truth and they develop the valuable gift of expressing themselves theologically. A senior Christian man normally takes the 'chair' and a question is proposed for the members of the group to discuss. Typical questions might be: 'Did Adam know he was a public person before he sinned?' 'When Christ said, "It is finished!", what was finished?' 'What is "liberty" in prayer?' This meeting of kindred minds leads to enriching insights for the whole group.

3.   *The pulpit should encourage the practice of spiritual conversation among members of a congregation.* A preacher may do this by throwing out one or two questions for the people to meditate on and discuss among themselves during the week, or else some passage of Scripture to explain. R. M. M'Cheyne used to do this. He would give out from the pulpit some text or chapter to think about. The fruits of the people's study and meditation might then be gleaned during a group meeting in the week, when mistakes could be corrected and valuable insights shared.

4.   *Particularly on the Lord's Day, Christians should endeavour to spend*

most of their free time in meditating on and speaking about spiritual subjects.
If the Puritans' strictures are to be taken seriously, we must
believe that 'unnecessary thoughts, words or works about our
worldly employments or recreations' [*Shorter Catechism* 61] are forbidden by the fourth commandment.

The great Christians of the past have striven to make the
Lord's Day a heaven on earth and to weave as much of Christ
into their conversation and meditation as they could. They sometimes did this in a way which was far from 'heavy'. For instance,
Archbishop Ussher once said to a friend, 'A word about Christ
ere we part.' More forcibly, Calvin declares, 'Every man ought to
withdraw himself from everything but the consideration of God
and his works [i.e. on the Lord's Day], that all men may be stirred
up to serve and honour him' [*Sermon 93 on Deuteronomy 15*].

On the other hand, deeply spiritual minds are particularly
grieved by trivial and worldly conversation on God's day. David
Brainerd, speaking of those who talked about secular matters on
the Sabbath, wrote in his Journal: 'Oh, I thought what a hell it
would be to live with such men to eternity.' A large part of the
due sanctification of the Lord's Day consists in restricting our
thoughts and words very specially to divine and spiritual subjects
and omitting unnecessary talk about ordinary things .

In conclusion, it needs to be said that there is a special blessing
attached to godly and spiritual conversation. To this Malachi
alludes in his prophecy: 'Then they that feared the Lord spake
often one to another: and the Lord hearkened, and heard it,
and a book of remembrance was written before him for them
that feared the Lord, and that thought upon his name' [*Mal.*
3:16]. What a promise! If Christians today were seriously to prac-
tise the pattern of this verse, how much more of God's presence
we should enjoy! Then let us study to edify one another. Those
who do so will discover that even the Almighty himself gives ear.

16

A Dose of Moral Courage

Scarcely anything in our modern society is so unwelcome as a moral judgement or a spiritual pronouncement. Evils of all sorts must be explained without reference to ethics or to God. This has reached a point close to absurdity whenever AIDS, for example, is referred to in the media. There is a studied attempt to prescribe ways of curtailing the spread of this disease which avoids all open reference to the real moral evil in man's life. None, it seems, dare grasp the nettle by saying that there is a Cause behind the curse. To suggest, as Paul does in Romans 1, that God has visited man's irregularity of life with a condign punishment is to commit a social crime and to raise Cain. So a veil of dissimulation has to be thrown over all the scandals of modern life. Anything which might look like a divine judgement is thus processed and conveniently laundered into non-ethical and non-judgemental categories.

One besetting sin of many religious spokesmen is their readiness to play this very same charade which the unbelieving world has invented. The main rule of the game is to avoid upsetting anyone's conscience. To be successful at such modern religious 'communication' (the term so much in vogue) one must become an expert in shadow-boxing with ecclesiastical fists. It reminds one forcibly of men jousting with balsa-wood lances or fighting with plastic swords that cannot draw blood.

A perfect specimen of how to fence and always miss your mark is to be found in two ARCIC statements which were drawn up as a basis for marriage between the Anglican and Roman Catholic churches.[1] There ought to have been issued with these sophistical statements a key to tell the reader how to transpose the sweetness and light into theological truth and historical reality. The tortuous steps backwards, forwards, up and down, now this side and now that, are the only things that betray the unmentionable fact that the two dancing-partners are neither used to one another's embrace nor trustful of one another's movements. The whispered conversation between the two lovers would amuse us if there were not stupendous issues at stake: 'Here we both are at long last—you and I. In the past we had great disagreements, of course. But that was all because we did not truly understand one another. *Now* we know that we both really meant the same things all the time. Let us both talk in carefully coded speech and our people will never know what we are doing till the deed is done. You will not really mind the Pope being at the head, will you?'

There is among all sorts of persons a crying need to take a dose of moral courage. The need is not for more cleverness or more education, nor for more analysis or more research into man's problems. It is for more straightforward speaking. It is for more openness. It is for more boldness to call things what they are and to set them in the light of God's Word. The man who will courageously refuse to play the popular game of deception is the man who will win the title of prophet to this generation.

This is what every pulpit should be doing. It is the glory of the pulpit that there a man speaks as the interpreter of heaven's mind, no matter what the world may say. Our people come to God's house weary. Their minds have been numbed by the secular argument which eliminates God and anaesthetizes moral judgement. When they come to the congregation, they thirst for renewed ethical and spiritual rearmament. The task of the pulpit is to sharpen blunted convictions in those who hear us and to renew their confidence in the things they have believed out of God's Word. There are many things which may make a preacher tone down his message. He may be afraid of those denominational leaders who wield the cudgels of power. Or he may have a cowardly fear of disturbing the peace, though he knows perhaps that beneath the surface of the congregation there lies an abundance of rottenness and death. Or he may be a career man who wants to climb to the top at the price of a treasonable silence. Every age spawns such men.

Whatever weaknesses a minister may have, however, let him not be spineless. A spineless prophet is a contradiction in terms and an unnatural monster. Society and the modern church alike both need to hear the prophetic voice of men who can call evil and sin by their proper names. They need men whose sermons will lift their hearers above the here-and-now to the great transcendental realities of God's ultimate judgement, and will in that way show the conscience what God thinks of his wayward world. The pulpit's task is to declare the sinfulness of sin and the one divine remedy for its removal.

It may be wondered whether one pulpit in a thousand is doing its God-given work as it should. There is too little thunder. The lion's roar is absent. Too few sermons smite with the fist of biblical certainty or call for a break with conventional religious vices. Most sermons of the day suffer from chronic anaemia and betray too much the taste of this present world.

What is the malady that has left the churches dumb while moral and spiritual wickedness is so rampant? Is it not at two points that this disease must be examined?

1.   The Christian needs to be reminded that there is no loss on earth more deadly than the loss of religious *conviction*. It is not enough that truth be held in the head. It must be held in the heart and in the soul. That is what makes all the difference. Are we ready to stand up and declare the truth because it is the truth? Are we ready to suffer for the truth? Have we *loved* the truth? It is the love of the truth which God demands of his people [*2 Thess.* 2:10]. That is what real Calvinism and real Puritanism stand for. Indeed, that is what real Christianity itself is.

2.   The Christian needs to be reminded that if ever men forsake the love of the truth, they fall under God's judgement. There is a sore punishment for disliking the truth. God sends upon such people a 'strong delusion, that they should believe a lie' [*2 Thess.* 2:11]. When men are judicially blinded in this manner, they become fit to turn black into white. The Roman mass can now be interpreted as only the Holy Eucharist under an alien name. Mary becomes the Mother of God and Mediatrix of our salvation. The ministry becomes the priesthood. All churches are just one. So truth stands on its head and theology is made to seem nonsense. Our Protestant Reformers are now simply said to have 'misunderstood' the teaching of the Council of Trent concerning justification! And the Church of Rome is now said to have anathematized the teaching of the Reformers because they did not quite appreciate their nuances! Similarly, society today fudges the ethical questions relating to AIDS, abortion, the guilt of criminal behaviour . . . The list is endless. The plague has already begun.

O for a dose of moral courage! Let preachers take the lead and let the people follow. And may God arise in his grace to deliver us all.

17
Glorying in Our Infirmities

It is a sign of passing beyond the stage of infancy in the life of grace when we have learned to glory in infirmities. The apostle Paul tells us that this was a leading feature of his life: 'Most gladly therefore will I rather glory in my infirmities, that the power of Christ may rest upon me' [*2 Cor.* 12:9]. It is an aspect of the spiritual life which calls for some attention.

The apostle Paul himself evidently had to be divinely taught before he learned to glory in infirmities. He tells us that the lesson came home to him as the result of a God-sent discipline on his life. His sublime experience of being raised to the third heaven needed to be counterbalanced by the subsequent discomfort of a thorn in his flesh. He tells us that he prayed three times for the removal of this 'thorn' and that Christ refused to grant him his request.

As a consequence, the apostle was obliged to go on suffering as a result of this mysterious (and, surely, physical) affliction. But it was God's way of leading him to see the entire life of grace in a new light. He perceived that there lies a paradox at the very heart of all true Christian experience. He states it in different ways to make the point clearer to us. 'Of myself I will not glory, but in mine infirmities' [*2 Cor.* 12:5]. 'Therefore I take pleasure in infirmities . . . for Christ's sake' [v.10]. 'When I am weak, then am I strong' [v.10]. This is the strange paradox of a healthy Christian mentality. It refuses to glory in its own strengths and prefers to make an admission of its own weaknesses. The mentality here described is the genuinely and consistently Christian one, argues Paul, because it rests upon this theological principle: Christ's 'strength is made perfect in weakness' [*2 Cor.* 12:9].

When believers glory in their strong points, therefore, they must expect Christ to withdraw his grace from them in some measure. Alternatively, when Christians 'glory in infirmities', they make a kind of appeal to Christ to be their compensation. Christ sublimates, as it were, the losses and crosses of his people in this life. In confessing their weaknesses, believers are warranted to expect that the Lord will infuse into their souls an additional degree of grace to sustain them in their felt weakness and need.

Such appears to be the substance of what Paul is stating. It is a principle of great importance to believers in the cultivation and development of their spiritual life. Indeed, it may be said to be one of the greatest secrets of Christian sanctification. If we appreciate Paul's inspired insight in this passage of Scripture, we shall have made an important step forward.

WHY THIS MENTALITY IS RARE

It would appear that Paul's mentality is rare. One meets rather more professing Christians who glory in their strengths than in their weaknesses. It is not difficult to see why this should be so. We all have a powerful urge to make a good impression on others. The language of man's heart is: 'I will be thought to be something.' It is right to wish to be high in God's service and kingdom. But it is weakness to wish to seem to be important merely in the estimation of other men.

Grace modifies the tendency, but it does not eliminate it in this life. Consequently, the impulse to promote ourselves in the eyes of others may sometimes take on, after conversion, only a different current. 'I will be well thought of in this church or in this fellowship, or among these other ministers'! 'I will not have people fail to think me important as a deacon, as an elder, as a preacher'! It is not enough to our proud heart to be esteemed by God. We would much prefer to be well thought of by our fellows also.

Of course, no man, unless he is a fool, would dream of letting his thoughts out to others so frankly as this. But there are coded ways of saying such things. A man may glory in himself without departing from the accepted conventions of evangelical parlance. With a few deft strokes, it is easy for the tongue to tell whom we know and where we have preached, what we have witnessed by our means and what progress the work has made ever since we came into it, where we expect to reach in a year's time and how many we know of who are recently added to the church . . . No serpent suns himself more proudly than fallen man in the warmth of his own importance.

This tendency is in every Christian, even the best. Its presence in our hearts should be a constant source of mortification and horror to us. Every time we feel this urge to glory in ourselves rising up from our corruptions, we need to cry out inwardly to God for forgiveness and fresh mercy. 'If thou hast done foolishly in lifting up thyself, or if thou hast thought evil, lay thy hand upon thy mouth' [*Prov.* 30:32]. Proud thoughts cry to God for a humbling and the wise in heart will flee in alarm to Christ, the city of refuge, before the chastisement can overtake him. It is a daily, hourly battle.

That the holiest and best Christians have felt the life-long need to mortify their own pride is very plain to see in their diaries, journals and 'day-books'. Such expressions as the following are commonplace: 'Do not bring the match of praise too close to me, for I carry a powder-keg in my own heart.' 'My heart is tinder; keep away the flame of flattery!' 'I love men's praise—and hate myself for loving it!' 'A pope is in my own soul.' 'The devil told me that was a good sermon before you did!' It does not make a man into a Uriah Heep to glory in infirmities. On the contrary, it strengthens his whole soul and toughens his fibre for spiritual effort.

IGNORANCE OF GOD'S WAYS

There appears to be a still deeper reason why some give themselves liberty to glory in themselves and in their supposed strengths. It is surely because they have somehow picked up a false perception of God's ways. It is a theological fault learned from worldly men. By the men of this world it is believed that they must promote *themselves* if they are to be successful in life. It is almost the only way to 'get on' in this world for men to 'sell themselves'. That is the world's way—to project an image, create an impression and make a fair showing in the flesh of one sort or another. No worldly man really admires or emulates Christian self-effacement, which is considered to be an 'under-selling' of oneself. In this world, therefore, image, style and such-like things are thought to be all-important. Not only businessmen and actors but also politicians and presidents are under pressure to conform to these requirements of the worldly mind.

It is all too easy for God's people to become conformed to this way of thinking and reasoning. The motive may be good. It is done to advance God's work. No cause could be more vital. So we become conditioned into thinking that we must play the world's game. We must sell the gospel! We must appear successful! Insidiously, yet as sure as destiny, the church falls into the trap of glorying in its strength. Weaknesses are papered over. Shortcomings are left unmentioned. 'God is doing a good work here!'

is all the cry. The motive is good; but there lies at the root of all such 'big talk' a worm of ignorance which will prove fatal if not detected in time.

If we are to take Paul the apostle for our guide, we must avoid glorying in ourselves and in our strong points as we would avoid a plague. That was what the false apostles of Paul's day were doing. It was what *he* refused to do at all costs. Paul tells us the reason why he will glory only in his weaknesses, infirmities, trials and sorrows. It is so that 'the power of Christ may rest' upon him [2 Cor. 12:9]. And may that not be a good part of the answer to the question, so often asked in our days: 'Why have we so little power?' Paul evidently did not go out of his way to impress men with his image! 'His bodily presence is weak and his speech contemptible' [2 Cor. 10:10]. This is the way his critics could refer to him. He would not have made a film star. 'I . . . came not with excellency of speech or of wisdom declaring unto you the testimony of God' [1 Cor. 2:1]. He was not a showy speaker. Evidently he did not consider the gospel's interests to be promoted by attending assiduously to the 'outward appearance' [2 Cor. 10:7]. He had to bear with the charge of being 'rude in speech' [2 Cor. 11:6]. It seems that to some he was unimpressive even in his delivery as a preacher. Only with considerable embarrassment could he be prevailed on to refer to his ministerial labours and privileges [2 Cor. 12:11].

On the other hand, he readily gloried in his infirmities because he had learned by experience and by revelation from God that when he did so 'the power of Christ' rested on him [2 Cor. 12:9].

Is it not here at this very point that Paul was so strong and many are so weak? 'The power of Christ'! What is that, but the power of Christ's grace to sweeten life, to sanctify affliction, to purify the soul, to brighten our hopes, to gladden our hearts and even to give unction to our preaching? Here is the needed dimension! But so long as the church glories in itself, we forfeit this blessing. To project our 'better side' for all the world to see, is to drive out the abiding presence of Christ. But without Christ's indispensable power to bless us and to make us 'able ministers of the new testament' [*2 Cor.* 3:6] we are nothing.

The conclusion seems inescapable. The way to grow in strength is to diminish in self-importance. The way to enjoy more of Christ in our lives is to be more honest, more realistic about what we are and less obsessed with the urge to keep up appearances with other people at all costs.

18

Satan's Advantages From Christians' Frailties

There must be something approaching joy among the
devils in hell just as there is joy among evil men in this
world. The joy of angels and Christian persons arises from
their receiving news of sinners repenting and turning to God.
The joy (if we may call it that) of devils springs from their witnessing anything which appears to damage the cause of God or
to wound and weaken the witness of his people upon earth.

We suppose that the devil and his angels find satisfaction
through the triumphing of evil in the measure in which such evil
is promoted by godly men. That evil should be advanced by
faithless and ungodly men of this world, therefore, must afford
to demons a satisfaction at the lower end of the scale. But when,
through infirmity or prejudice, *godly* persons do Satan's work for
him, this—we may reasonably suppose—is the pinnacle and
summit of Satan's joy.

There can be no doubt that Satan employs immense
resources of time, skill and effort to win over persons with
influence in God's kingdom to do him service. There is more
evidence in the Bible for this than one might at first suppose.
The general rule of operation used by Satan, it would appear, is

the obvious one of striking against God by means of his closest friends and most honoured servants. In this way Satan endeavours to inflict as great a blow against heaven as possible and to injure God's work from the least-expected quarter.

In all this, let it be said, we do not forget that God's purpose is eternal and inviolable. But we draw attention to the love of cunning and 'subtlety' [*Gen.* 3:1], the serpentine and crooked [*Isa.* 27:1] way in which Satan is fond of working. It is this 'cunning craftiness' [*Eph.* 4:14] which is the distinctive hall-mark of all his age-old industry of duplicity against the people of God. Satan's joy, to put it plainly, is most seen in his using God's best instruments against Himself.

The above observations are surely borne out by the evidence. When Satan would murder mankind at a stroke he employed as his best ally the wife of Adam, our covenant-head. Here was the world's first and purest lady and the mother of mankind. We all fell in Adam. But it was through the woman given to be his greatest earthly blessing that Adam was induced to murder all his posterity. What satisfaction it must have been to the tempter that he got 'the mother of all living' to be the first instrument in their death! No mother's love was so perfect as hers—and no temptation so deadly as hers.

We see the same dark hand at work as soon as God had formed Israel into a covenanted people to himself. Even while Moses is still on Sinai receiving the Ten Commandments, Satan is busy fostering apostasy among the people. This he does, not by means of some outsider, but by the hand of Aaron, Moses' brother, on whose authority the golden calf is made. Could any craft have been more crafty or could any mischief have been more mischievous? While the one brother serves God on the holy mount, the other serves Satan beneath its shadow. Even as the finger of God engraves the second commandment in letters of stone, the very brother of Moses himself is at work graving an idol to cause the people to break it! The subtlety is too great to emanate from any other mind than that of Satan. The irony in wickedness is stamped all over with the serpent's image.

The same pattern is visible in the career of Saul, the first king. Here is a man who receives his kingship very definitely from God himself [*1 Sam.* 10]. If any man in history could claim to sit on a throne by 'divine right' (to use a phrase much loved by Stuart kings), it was Saul the son of Kish. How ironical then that such a king should be a disaster both to himself and to the people of God! What a joy there was in hell when Saul, the anointed of the Lord, consulted with the witch of Endor and, next day, died ignominiously on the field of battle! 'Tell it not in Gath' was David's mournful reaction. It was too tragic not to be one of Satan's special stratagems.

We may well suppose that the crucifixion of Christ at the hands of his Jewish countrymen is the supreme irony ever fostered by the devil. It is history's perfect masterpiece of hellish subterfuge because it is history's greatest crime and it was committed, alas, by the most devout and religious people history had ever known up to that time. That some hidden, and lurking power of spiritual wickedness lay behind the frenzied hatred of the Jews is plain to every reader of the Scriptures: 'This is your hour and the power of darkness' [*Luke* 22:53]. Our instinctive love for the Jews as a people only intensifies our sadness, when we reflect on the awful fact that 'he came unto his own, and his own received him not' [*John* 1:11]. In Christian compassion we long for the day when their insensate cry of 'His blood be on us and on our children!' will cease to call down judgement upon them and they as a people will receive the 'Spirit of grace and of supplications' and so will 'look on him whom they have pierced' [*Zech.* 12:10] in repentance and faith.

That Peter did the devil's work handsomely on one occasion is further evidence that Satan always seeks to use the friends closest to God to do his work for him. The lessons which flow to us from the words of Christ on the occasion in question are full of solemn instruction and warning to every minister, elder, church and Christian. Christ's 'Get thee behind me, Satan' [*Matt.* 16:23] leaves us in no doubt that the best of Christians, the best of preachers, the holiest of saints and the most intimate of Christ's friends may, all unwittingly, do the devil's work for him at times. That they do it unconsciously and with the purest of motives goes far to excuse them in our eyes. But this very sincerity makes their influence all the more likely to do harm where they are most convinced they are doing only good.

As if to intensify our awareness of the fact that spiritual harm may spring up to the followers of Christ where least expected, God ordained and fore-warned that the traitor who should betray the Lord Jesus Christ was none other than one of his chosen apostles. This came as a surprise to the twelve when they first heard it and it is entirely understandable that they would proceed to enquire, 'Lord, is it I?' [*Matt.* 26:22]. We are certainly not less gullible today than they were in their day and therefore we too have to take account of the possibility that those most closely associated with the work of Christ's gospel may become the betrayers of it before their course is fully run. From this possibility no one is exempt. 'Watch and pray' is our only antidote. Even then we need further to examine ourselves, to search our motives and to lay bare our hearts before the scrutiny of Almighty God.

It is awesome to see how, in the course of church history, Satan has taken advantage of the flaws in understanding or practice which God's eminent servants have had. From the brilliant Origen came the allegorical interpretation of Scripture. From the courageous Athanasius, with his respect for Antony and the life of solitude, came the ideal of a monastic Christianity. From the inexactitudes of the toweringly great Augustine emanated the medieval theory of sacramentalism. From the organizing zeal of Cyprian and Ambrose developed the later hierarchical structures of the papal church. The devil has proved masterful in exploiting the excesses or shortcomings, the over-enthusiasm or thoughtless incaution of eminent preachers and churchmen in the past. No doubt they aimed at perfection in all things. But in that they missed the mark they gave occasion to Satan to push their errors to undreamed of lengths. This he has done contrary to their intentions at the time, but by a skilful use of their respected names and using their authority among all the lovers of orthodoxy.

Let no man think that this aspect of the devil's duplicity ended with the Church Fathers. It has gone on ever since and remains one of the most successful weapons against the church. Hence we must not only watch our weaknesses, but our strengths as well. The vices of our virtues are more generally harmful to the cause of Christ than our observed vices. It happens in all kinds of ways.

One man, let us say, becomes an internationally important evangelist. He quite naturally and rightly seeks to bring his influence to bear on the largest possible number of people. He is sound in the basic elements of gospel truth, a Bible-lover and a man of God. He is zealous to win as many souls to Christ as he can. But a dilemma faces him. His conservative theology is resented by Liberals and Catholics. What is he to do?

The confrontational approach will result in smaller crowds at his meetings. Is it not right in the interests of reaching these very persons, to give them some say in the conduct and order of the religious services? At the very least, can some pleasant and softening speeches not be made to win their attachment to the campaigns? If the evangelist of our illustration does so (and let us believe the best of his motives) he is guilty of taking a false step and of committing grave error. By this one false move he now wields all his considerable influence and prestige in the direction of blurring the lines between truth and falsehood. But he may live and die without realizing what he has done. The devil, meanwhile, is not slow to draw the threads of falsehood all the more firmly around the minds of those many thousands who, quite understandably, lionized the evangelist.

The above is only one example out of many in which Satan exploits the infirmities of believers. There are applications to every congregation, every denomination, every pulpit and every pew. We might suffer this patiently without additional comment except that in certain cases the advantage gained by Satan becomes so great that it cries out for the utmost attention before it carries everything before it.

Such a situation was reached in the last century with the rise of the Higher Critical theory. It may well be that some of those who joined in the stampede for a critical approach to the text of Holy Scripture were men with grace and good intention. If so, they were tragically misled, as the sequel has proved. But we know ourselves too well to forget that we all go astray 'like sheep' [*Isa.* 53:6]. That is to say, we all incline too much towards following others. We love a leader who will do our thinking for us and go over the new ground before us. The price we pay is that we occasionally follow our leaders even over the enchanted ground, and we may have gone some way before we realize our danger and are able with pain and humiliation to find our way back to the path.

There is one supremely important practical lesson to be learnt from the way Satan takes advantage of the infirmities of

135

Christians. It is that we should seek always to attach the blame for the mischief which occurs rather to him than to them. Satan is expert at starting fires with other men's matches and leaving them to get the blame for it. If our gifted leaders get us into some troubles on occasion, we must have the grace to give them the benefit of the doubt and believe them to be acting on good motives. That their overemphasis or excess of zeal or want of forethought led them into making imprudent decisions or to cracking the nut with a sledge-hammer, we must not forget that the mischief which ensued was far more Satan's work than theirs.

It goes without saying also that wise leadership should always realise that it is capable of carrying a good thing too far and giving a handle unwittingly to the common adversary of our souls. Our universal folly as sinners is to become too much like ourselves, to the point where we love ourselves even for our own extremes. But this is an infirmity, and one which Satan will assuredly exploit to hurt the general cause of Christ. A paraffin lamp gives a tolerably good light if the wick is adjusted correctly. But if the wick is turned up too far it sends forth only smoke. Even so do our strong points help our brothers and sisters greatly. But, if strained and stretched too far, our helpful emphases only darken the fellowship and offend the believers. Happy are we if we distrust our own hearts enough to accept correction from those who love us in the Lord.

19

Where Have the Saints Gone?

S in has had two remarkable effects on our critical powers. It has made us super-sensitive to the faults of others and insensitive to our own. We are born experts at seeing the shortcomings of our neighbour. But a spiritual long-sightedness renders us oblivious to the same shortcomings in ourselves. Why is it so much easier for us to advise our brother of the speck in his eye than to remove the beam from our own? 'Show me myself' is not a common prayer.

'Know thyself' has been a maxim of the philosophers and sages from early times. But, for all that, which of them really knew himself? Robert Burns was no saint but he felt the need to exclaim:

> O wad some Pow'r the giftie gie us
> To see oursels as others see us!

Burns sighed, as we all sigh in our better moments, at the sobering realization that self-knowledge is that form of knowledge which we attain to last.

The consciousness that we are partly unknown to ourselves is fully confirmed by the Word of God. 'Who can understand his errors?' asks David [*Ps.* 19:12]. 'All the ways of a man are clean in his own eyes; but the Lord weigheth the spirits,' affirms Solomon

[*Prov.* 16:2]. 'Therefore thou art inexcusable, O man,' argues the apostle Paul, 'whosoever thou art that judgest: for wherein thou judgest another, thou condemnest thyself; for thou that judgest doest the same things . . . And thinkest thou this, O man, that judgest them which do such things, and doest the same, that thou shalt escape the judgment of God?' [*Rom.* 2:1, 3]. It was to his own people and not to strangers that our Lord could say, 'Ye know not what manner of spirit ye are of' [*Luke* 9:55]. These texts have something in them for us all.

Protestants we may be, and Evangelicals we may be, but into our Protestantism and into our evangelicalism we each import a hidden something which belongs to neither but is the blind spot in our own personal religion.

FROM EXTREME TO EXTREME

Every generation of Christians has its besetting sins. Ours is no exception. Perhaps we should say that we witness today an abuse of biblical principles among Christians not very different from the abuses of the medieval church in its own peculiar way. Medieval Christianity, with its monkish cells and hours of solitary introspection, represented the movement of the pendulum to one extreme. We, however, have erred in swinging to the opposite extreme. They made religion to consist solely of meditation. We have produced a type of Christianity that is all extrovert and which has little or no interest in the cultivation of the soul. The medieval Christians were morbid; we have idolized 'happiness'. They abandoned preaching for praying; we have made 'witnessing' everything. They fled from 'the world'; we live in it and we are in danger of urging too far the principle of 'Christian liberty' for being too much in it and too much like it.

We in our day see the folly of medieval monks and we are right to deplore their extremism, their false view of the world, their failure to preach to sinners, their superstitious theology—in a word, their inability to see their own shortcomings. It is humbling and salutary therefore for us to recall that the next age of believers will in its day write a history of our own times and will do so with that perception of *our* sinfulness which now eludes us because we live too close to ourselves to see it.

OUR MORTAL WOUND

If we could see ourselves as we should, what would we see? 'What is the glaring fault of the modern Christian?' we might ask. It is our duty to ask it. Is there one thing more than another which is conspicuous by its absence in Christian circles today? Given that we all come short in all things, what in particular are we to look to as the gravest wound in the modern church's body? We may comfort ourselves that the fault is not in our Reformation principles. The modern Calvinist has a notional theology which surpasses all the theologies of the Middle Ages and of the early church. Reformation principles are not our weakness but our tower of strength. No siren voice which urges us to soften our Puritan creeds, either by subtraction or addition, deserves a moment's attention. The fault is not in our creed. It lies elsewhere.

Again, knowledge, ability and articulation are not our mortal wound. The contemporary Christian mind is informed from a hundred sources. We analyse, evaluate, comment and discuss. There is not a continent and scarcely a mission field of which we are ignorant. All doctrine comes under our review. We are meticulously well informed. Our weakness is not in information. It is elsewhere.

Where have all the saints gone? Surely we live in an age in which Christianity has parted company with holiness. Religion has become a thing rather of the mind than of the soul. Provided a man can say the right things, knows the right language, makes the right noises, hc passes muster for a Christian. There is little demand made of modern Christians to 'work out' their 'own salvation'. Fear of God is rare. Not many rise above the level of being 'ordinary'.

What we need, besides better preaching, is better living. Our attitude towards the Reformers, Puritans and early Methodists is rather one of wonderment at their amazing spirituality than a serious attempt to emulate it. We have somehow isolated those aspects of our Reformed heritage which we find congenial and have left unattempted those parts which are irksome to flesh and blood. The result is that when we call ourselves 'Reformed' we too often mean that we have embraced a set of theological ideas rather than the holier type of life that once went with them. The first we should do without leaving the second undone.

THE CULTIVATION OF THE SOUL.
Generally speaking, churches, seminaries and Christian movements are only as good as the persons who are in them. They will rise no higher than the level of their leaderships and memberships. The truth of the gospel is the same in every age. It is a constant factor. What varies so greatly is the human factor that accompanies it.

Admittedly, it is what we preach rather than what we are that will turn the world upside down. But if we preach what we conspicuously are not then we do no more than bring the truth into contempt. Sadly this aspect of the modern church has been highlighted in the case of some American television evangelists in recent times. Scripture should teach us, and if not, then painful experience will teach us, that God will not normally bless even his own truth when it is held with a bad conscience and with an unrighteous life. Good doctrine with bad living does not lead to the spread of Christianity but to a society which becomes sceptical and eventually pagan. There are not lacking signs that this process is already at an advanced stage in lands once famous for the gospel.

Where do we begin, if we mean to repair the ruin we see all around us? Surely there can be only one answer. We must pay more attention to the soul. Holiness begins with the 'inner man' and proceeds outwards to every aspect of life. The soul is the man himself. Neither sound confession nor larger libraries nor anything else will preserve our churches from the sins of this age if we ourselves do not become better men and women.

There will be no marked growth in Christian holiness if we do not labour to overcome our natural disinclination towards secret spiritual exercises. Our forefathers kept honest diaries where the soul's battles were recorded. Thomas Shepard, Pilgrim Father and founder of Harvard, wrote in his private papers, 'It is sometimes so with me that I will rather die than pray.' So is it with us all. But this honesty is not commonplace. Such men climbed high only as they laboured with sweat and tears to cultivate the soul. We, too, must 'exercise ourselves unto godliness' [*1 Tim.* 4:7].

There is a good to be got from our spiritual exercises which nothing will make up for if neglected. It is in soaking our spirits daily in Scripture to the point of fatigue and in daily secret wrestlings with the Almighty to the point of tears and crying that the soul is made strong. Even Christ himself was not exempted from the necessity of such regular experiences of anguish in his devotions [*Heb.* 5:7-8]. We recoil from the challenge which such a passage beckons us to enter. But all the great souls of our Reformed and Puritan tradition, and some in less privileged traditions too, have found the secret of the Lord as they learned to wait in his presence.

Where have the saints gone? There is no substitute for godliness. It is the best thing that can be said of any man when it can be said of him that he is 'a man of God'. Great spiritual movements begin when men take seriously the claims of truth upon themselves and their churches. Truth has a chemistry all of its own. It has a way of transforming the ordinary mind and the average tongue into instruments of awful power for God. It is not only the geniuses of history whom God has used to begin a revival. It has often been men of modest talent, yet men who had a surpassing personal knowledge of God, learned in the secret place and made molten with the holy desire to do something which would make the mountains tremble. Real holiness is not the pale and passive medieval kind but that which kindles with a consuming passion in the regenerate soul and cries, in the face of our decadent and indifferent society, 'Let God arise! I shall give thee no rest, O Lord, till thou come!' Such saints this world sorely needs. Perhaps more now than ever.

20

Where Godliness is Leaking

A religious movement is of value only in the measure in which it changes people's lives for the better. The mere holding of meetings, let us say, or the printing of books or else the organizing of congregations, camps, conferences and committees is of little worth if it does not lead to godly living on the part of those influenced by such enterprises. The holy life is the end in view of all true religious activity and it is its ample reward and justification. Wherever and whenever a religious movement ceases to produce the spiritual mind and the God-fearing life it has become a spent force. Whatever men may say in defence of such a movement's being continued, it is questionable whether it has the sanction or the blessing of heaven. History is strewn with examples of churches and organizations which began well and did good but which then departed from their original good work. Our own day with its many Christian movements and enterprises is no different from the past.

But it sometimes happens the other way round too. Sound churches and good organizations may suffer because, though they are doing the work of God faithfully, men do not live up to their privileges but learn to take the grace of God for granted. Many a good preacher feels like a man who is forever pouring water into a bucket full of holes. He empties out gallons of truth into men's ears over the space of a year, but he seems to see scarcely a spoonful of it taking effect in people's lives.

It is to be feared that there is a culpable leakage in our churches and fellowships. Many who attend Reformed and evangelical churches make little or no attempt to live up to the level of their church creeds and confessions. Many parents who hear sound preaching take marvellously little pains to see that their children are brought to a knowledge of salvation. Many parents who sit under the sound of the gospel do disappointingly little to order their homes and their family life in accordance with the principles of Holy Scripture. Between the pulpit and the pew there is a leakage to be seen which saps the life of churches and fellowships and which ought to be taken more seriously.

GODLINESS QUICKLY LOST

Godliness is soon lost. It is a delicate plant. A great preacher does not always have spiritual sons and does not often have spiritual grandsons. The saintly parent cannot guarantee godliness in his children, still less in his grandchildren. Holiness is vulnerable in this world. It is like snow that is quickly melted or mist which disperses when the sun rises up. In one single generation of a family or of a church the power of godliness which it previously had may be lost totally.

If we are to maintain and preserve the spirituality of our homes and churches we must act decisively and purposefully. This we shall not be prepared to do unless we are first convinced of the fact that godliness is the greatest blessing we can wish for our children and for all others over whom God gives us influence. We ought therefore to begin with the conviction that neither health nor happiness, wealth nor education, nor any other thing is comparable in importance to knowledge of God. If our children, our families and our congregations are poor in all else yet rich in their love to God, they are rich indeed. But if they are rich in all else and poor in love to Christ, they are miserably poor indeed. There can be no doubt that this is God's view of the matter and that it ought therefore to be ours also.

GODLINESS IN THE FAMILY

Not all Christians who have families have Christian families. There are families where Christians live but where the distinctives of a truly Christian home are absent. This is so where parents go to church but leave their children unnecessarily at home. It is so where meal-times are not sanctified by 'the word of God and prayer' [*1 Tim.* 4:5]. It is so where there is no proper order, no discipline and obedience, no reasonable punctuality, no respect for parents, no prominence given to the things of God except in a purely nominal way or where there is no sanctification of the Lord's Day above other days.

It should be the delight and the ambition of young Christians, when they become parents, to set up a home which is Christian in every sense. This is not done merely by hanging scenes from John Bunyan on all the walls. It begins with the cultivation of love, truth and respect between the members of the home. The parents must pull together, speak well to one another and speak well of one another. The husband, as head of the home, must 'rule' the house by his general bearing and demeanour as a man of abounding affection and good sense whose leadership is of proven worth and whose judgement is known to be formed by his extensive knowledge of the Word of God.

Such a man does not need normally to shout or to act heavy-handedly. He is loved and esteemed by all around him. Though they may sometimes behave playfully or take good-humoured advantage of him in slighter matters where no principles are at stake, as soon as he is seen to be in earnest every other member of the family must pay attention and treat his words with the gravity they deserve.

Similarly the wife of a Christian home must 'guide' the household and its affairs with a prudent regard to the well-being of each member and to the peace, unity and affection of the family as a whole. 'The hand that rocks the cradle rules the world.' No one can do a mother's part in life but the mother herself. It is her glory in the home that God has given her the first place of instinctive affection and intimacy with all her children. The children of the home need her even more than they need their father. Her influence for good is incomparable and she should exert all the energy she has to steer her children affectionately yet firmly in the ways of the Lord.

Generally speaking, the fault of Christian parents in this day is not to expect enough of their children in terms of the work and study which they do. We live in an age which is obsessed with sport, leisure and recreation. The Christian parent needs to correct this imbalance. The biblical ethic is in the words: 'six days shalt thou labour' [*Exod.* 20:9]. That is to say, work is the main business of life and play is very secondary. 'Bodily exercise profiteth little' [*1 Tim.* 4:8]. This attitude to life is 'according to godliness' and a wise parent will see that work, not play, is the main note in a child's developing outlook on life. Work is a blessing in many ways, not least because it leaves less room and strength for mischief and temptation. Similarly, a wise parent will put a stop to childish friendships outside the home which may not be for their child's spiritual or moral good.

Good parenting is vitally important for the good of the overall cause of God in the world. Not for nothing does the Bible tell us the names of the mothers of so many Old Testament kings. Most of us are either made or marred by our mothers. Good parenting can only be done by the parent. It cannot normally be

done by anyone else, though in families where special circumstances exist a godly relative or friend may play a minor role. It
is a thousand pities that most modern children come under
the dominant influence of a 'third parent' in the form of the
television set. Those Christian parents who allow their children
to watch television programmes habitually ought in conscience
to God and out of regard to their children's good to watch the
programmes with their children. It is the one sure way to
monitor what they see and hear.

Christian parents who use the television set as a regular 'child
minder' while they themselves attend to other things would
do well to ask themselves if they are really acting responsibly. Can
they be sure that while their back is turned the television is
not forming in the child's mind habits of thought and feeling
which will one day end in practical atheism? A child, let us
remind ourselves, may grow and develop perfectly well under the
impression of Bibles and books, without the supposed benefits
of those programmes which non-Christian families down the
street may look on as essential for their own children.

Every minister of the gospel today knows that godliness is
leaking badly in families where films and popular music are
allowed to control young lives. After all, children are only in
church two or three times a week. But the television and the
popular records are available every day when parents let it be
so. It was a good saying of an old divine: 'We have filled our
children's bones with original sin and we must spend all our
strength rooting it out.' There is nothing to compare, if godliness
is to be present in families, with the good old practice of holding
family worship morning and evening. The head of the family
gathers his wife and children about him while he reads a passage
of the Holy Scriptures, sings with them and prays for them. To
this practice should be added that of catechizing the young. It is

still possible for children to learn by heart the *Answers* to the Westminster Shorter Catechism or similar work. It may take the combined determination of parent and child to accomplish this feat. But it can be done and should be attempted. Even the less able child can be taught the catechism if enough parental care is taken. Even before a child can really speak it can be taught simple truths about God by means of story and picture.

What about the child in church? It astonishes many a preacher that parents do not go through the sermon afterwards with their children at home. At an early age children may be trained to listen for the text of a sermon and for the main headings, illustrations, etc. It might mortify many parents if they realized that their children hear scarcely anything a preacher says in his sermon, but are thinking their own thoughts! This is pardonable in the very young and in any event it is better that children should be in the house of God listening to preaching than not in church at all. But we ought as parents to gather up the crumbs for the young by asking them questions at home and by helping them to recall and to understand at least the rudiments of what the minister was preaching from God's Word.

HOW DO WE WORSHIP?

It goes without saying that a great part of godliness has to do with the attitude we form towards the worship of God. There are a number of areas where we might tighten up our modern approach to public worship. One such area is that of the gravity of our minds when we come to worship. It strikes us as very doubtful whether the Scriptures allow us to approach God's worship casually at any time, but especially not on the Lord's Day. The frequently repeated pronouncements of Scripture concerning our approach to him all lead to the conclusion that we need to put ourselves into a serious state of mind before and during every time of worship. The ineffable holiness and majesty of God demand that we come into his presence with awe and godly fear, with self-examination and self-abasement. These things will affect the way we speak and behave when we are in God's house. They will even be reflected in the way we dress and carry ourselves.

It is essential that there should be silence in the house of God during the worship. It may at times be tolerated if very young children utter babyish sounds. But it is not proper for parents to retain their children in the place of worship, during the sermon especially, if they are not able to keep them quiet. It occasionally happens that a parent has not the wisdom to realize this and needs to have it courteously pointed out to him or her by a responsible member of the congregation. But it ought not to happen. No preacher can compete with a crying baby and no congregation should allow the problem to arise.

Nothing which smacks of 'entertainment' is appropriate in the worship of God. Infinite harm is done when elements in a church service are aimed at amusing sinners rather than directing their minds to God. In some churches it has been a long-standing tradition to have certain 'lighter' events in the worship programme. But these, we believe, only mar and spoil God's worship and are not welcome to spiritual people. Laughter is not the appropriate response of a worshipping congregation. It is, we suggest, a pity when a congregation expects to laugh regularly in the course of a service of worship. We would do better if we controlled this spirit of mirth and kept it for other occasions.

THE CHRISTIAN'S SELF-WATCH
Christian character is largely formed, where it is correctly formed, in the secret place. This is why it is all-important for the believer to attend to his private devotions each day. No advice is

easier to give or harder to follow. There will, however, be no stopping the leakage of godliness unless we make conscience of our daily secret times of worship. It is as we meditate on the Word of God and hold communion with him in private prayer that the soul is transformed, we cannot say how, 'from glory to glory' [2 Cor. 3:18].

It is not so much what we say or what we know that counts for Christian character and influence as what we are. One man who is known for his sanctification and walks closely with Christ will be listened to when he utters a quiet rebuke more than another who speaks volubly and yet lacks a convincing life-style. There are talkers in plenty in every age. But those few who make a mark on their fellow-men for good are always the ones who have an indefinable 'something' about them which carries the stamp of authority and which arises from their nearness to God. Several of the spiritual duties which used to be regarded as normal and commonplace for earnest Christians have regrettably fallen out of fashion in recent years. We refer to the neglected practice of *learning passages of the Bible by heart,* not forgetting the psalms. If we are to be followers of the Reformers and Puritans in any sense of the word we must labour long and hard to master the Bible in our own language. It ought to be a matter of shame and regret to us not to know the text of the Bible better. If we cannot quote it then we are not Christians in 'complete armour' but in a semi-armed, and therefore semi-vulnerable, state.

This point is too often overlooked in all the modern debate about 'versions' of the Bible. It is not self-evident that those who enjoy the advantages (as they see them) of the more fashionable versions are able to quote the Bible more perfectly. The supreme need is that we should be full of the Scriptures, having them dwell plentifully in our hearts [Col. 3:16] so that we may combat the devil and so adorn the gospel with lives that are spiritual and sanctified.

A second point worth making about private devotions is that from time to time we might make it our policy to have *an extended period of prayer.* We probably all have our 'measure' in prayer. For some it is an hour daily. For many others it will be less, perhaps a lot less. By 'measure' we mean that extent of time spent in secret prayer which satisfies our soul and allows us opportunity to say to God more or less all we have to say at the time. More is expected of ministers in this respect. But all Christians are to spend a reasonable length of time in secret prayer.

What we here suggest is that it is very much for the advancement of godliness in ourselves and others that we should occasionally prolong our normal time of prayer. At seasons of felt need, for instance, we might well set aside a full hour or more for waiting on our knees before God. There are obvious and undoubted advantages in this practice. It is a way of *exercising* ourselves unto godliness [*1 Tim.* 4:7]. It 'stretches' the soul and enlarges its capacity. It deepens our seriousness. It calls forth an increased measure of grace from the Almighty. Too few, we fear, are the times when modern Christians pray or fast to the point of fatigue. But the psalmist knew such an experience: 'My knees are weak through fasting; and my flesh faileth of fatness' [*Ps.* 109:24].

A third suggestion for promoting godliness which our fore-fathers made good use of was the keeping of a religious diary, or 'day-book', as they would call it. There are numerous benefits to this practice. It teaches us to notice the daily providences of God—an oft-neglected yet rewarding duty [*Ps.* 107:42-43]. It teaches us to put spiritual thoughts, experiences and desires into appropriate words. It trains us to check and compare our progress today with our progress in the past. It shows how God

151

prompts us to prayer, hears prayer and eventually answers prayer. It will become a well-spring of comfort in hours of darkness. In short, the keeping of a daily record of our spiritual state will go a long way to enriching our life and advancing the great task of enjoying and glorifying God.

God has blessed us in this generation with a recovery of many glorious doctrines long buried under the rubbish of tradition and error. Our concern must be to 'improve' our privilege. Not to do that would be ingratitude to God. We owe it to Christ to be the best of Bible-readers and the best hearers of sermons. We owe it to our families and to posterity to see that the church children of this rising generation see the best examples and receive the best instruction. Then let it be our heartfelt wish to stop up the leaks between pulpit and pew, between the godliness of father and son, between what we are in our creeds and what we are in our lives. It is a subject in which great issues are at stake.

IV

Life Together

So we, being many, are one body in Christ,
and every one members one of another . . .
Let love be without dissimulation.
Abhor that which is evil;
cleave to that which is good.
Be kindly affectioned one to another
with brotherly love;
in honour preferring one another.

Romans 12:5, 9-10.

21

The Fellowship of Saints

Fellowship between Christians is the gift of God. It is a true means of grace. Christians are spiritual people and they feel comparatively isolated in this world. But God gives them this compensation, that the fellowship they enjoy with like-minded believers is marvellously therapeutic and sweet. Fellowship exists between all believers because they have the principal things in common: the experience of saving grace, the enmity of the world, the expectation of coming glory, a thirst for God, grateful love to Christ and acceptance of Holy Scripture.

Basic to the New Testament idea of fellowship is this very one of 'having things in common'. The Greek term is *koinōnia*. But to know the New Testament word does not give us the experience. The meaning of New Testament fellowship can only be known by us if we are spiritual and lively Christians. A great deal of what passes for 'fellowship' is often no more than human friendship such as men might have in a club or lodge. It is good and necessary but not equivalent to the precise thought conveyed in God's Word by the term 'fellowship'.

A believer's duty is to promote true fellowship by all the means open to him in this life. He should also regard it as his privilege and duty to improve the quality of his fellowship as far as he can. We probably do not do enough in our day to promote spiritual and edifying fellowship. And yet it is something which is most urgently needed; and that for obvious reasons.

Christians are lonely. They are scattered far from one another and are often kept exceptionally busy at their secular jobs. Consequently, they are spiritually very tired by the time they meet with one another, and are chronically in need of that comfort and nursing which only Christian company is able to give them. Not only so, but believers are today confused in all kinds of ways. They are frequently bewildered by the babel of false teachings, alarmed at the unfaithfulness of church leaders and perplexed by the rapid succession of changes in our modern world. Besides, a time of declension is always a weary time.

HINDRANCES TO FELLOWSHIP

Fellowship is understandably a delicate thing. After all, it consists of the interaction of human spirits upon one another in an atmosphere of trust and confidence. All the participants are sinful, even though saved, and all are more or less sensitive. All vary in gifts, education, articulation and sanctification. It is inevitable, therefore, that there must be an awareness among believers that certain things are to be avoided if fellowship is not to be hindered:

1. Fellowship is not improved by the presence of believers who *never attempt to talk about the truths of religion*. There are some professing Christians who can talk about anything and everything except the things of God. Sport, politics, economics and international relations may have a place in good men's conversations occasionally. But they are not the stuff of Christian fellowship. It is not apostolic Christianity to turn the gospel into an unmentionable secret. There is no government statute forbidding us to 'leak' the mysteries of the faith to one another when we gather into groups for mutual edification. Paul refers to

believers who 'in conference added nothing' [*Gal.* 2:6]. There are too many who, in a culpable sense, leave us in that condition.

2.   Fellowship is not enhanced by believers who have only one-stringed fiddles and *cannot talk about any subject except their own pet theme*. One-track-mindedness is an infirmity which leads other believers to groan inwardly while they are courteously smiling outwardly. The good man who always leads the conversation to the millennium, or the anti-Christ, or the superior merits of his own church ought to do his brothers and sisters the occasional service of 'changing the gramophone record'. Those fellowships which are dominated by small-mindedness will very quickly famish and sicken. The remedy is to do some fresh reading and to hunt for truths in pastures new. Attending a good Christian conference also helps to rub off the corners of prejudice.

3.   Fellowship is not promoted when one person commandeers the group in the belief that he is the *only one whose voice ought to be listened to*. A fellowship is not a monologue or a soliloquy, but an exercise in giving and taking. All should feel there is space enough in the speaking to get a few words in edgeways from time to time. All should be encouraged to feel that they have something worth saying. All should be left with the impression that they contributed their two mites to the general good, even if they were not so advanced or prolific in knowledge as most of their brothers and sisters. Christian love honours the lowly and makes the poorly gifted feel welcome.

4.   Again, we might notice that Christian fellowship is the poorer when *we relax so much that our tongue runs away with us*. Alas, we have all been guilty and have painful recollection of situations in which we spoke and laughed, jested and gossiped more like fools

than wise men. Our conscience faithfully told us so on the way home and no argument of our minds could convince us otherwise in the end.

5. On the other hand, *we must not be glum, sombre or depressing.* We should be generous to lonely Christians when they seem to 'let go' a little in good company. Christians must be able to find relief in fellowship. The human spirit will snap if it does not unbend at times. David danced before the ark. We must not, like Michal [2 *Sam.* 6:20], be sour or disapproving of what may be the spiritual ecstasy of the brethren when they meet one another.

To be circumspect is always our duty. But it is a blot on our fellowship when we become so morose or monkish that we leave no place for innocent and well-meant elation. The Harris blacksmith danced round his anvil when he heard that the 'apostle of the north', Dr John Macdonald of Ferintosh, was coming. To act the part of a 'wet blanket' may feel pious but it will be certain to quench that delight which is an essential ingredient of real fellowship.

PROMOTING FELLOWSHIP

These are some of the negatives. But what, we may ask on the positive side, are the best ways to promote and enrich our Christian fellowships so that they may be occasions of real blessing among one another? The following measures, it seems to us, deserve serious consideration:

1. It will help our fellowship meetings when we come together with *some well-prepared spiritual thoughts* to share with one another. Let each of the group keep a little manna by him in his pot which he can share with his fellows in company. This is to be the fruit of his own study, reading, meditation and recollection. And let us talk of the sermon! If those in the pews of evangelical churches

talked more about the contents of their ministers' preaching, they would get better sermons from their ministers.

2.   Fellowship is the place where *the religion of the heart is much promoted.* Here we draw forth from one another those deep counsels which lie hidden in the soul. Experiences of God in providence, enjoyment of God in secret, the answers to prayer, the hand of God in guidance—these are the matters on which true fellowship feeds. Because there is love and mutual confidence, we take one another's experiences on trust and we neither despise the elementary nor adulate the impressive. But we lay all to our heart in one way or another. Some men's experiences we covet and seek for ourselves. Others we prefer not to have. But we do not treat dismissively what God does with our brothers and sisters as though our own experiences were the rule or measure of all the church.

3.   Above all, *let us seek to have the felt sense of Christ's presence* with us when we gather together in fellowship. There is nothing more healthful to Christian hearts than the realization that there is a divine 'presence' with them. Those who dismiss such a thought as sentimental piety have a lot to learn about the meaning of Christ's promises: 'Where two or three are gathered together in my name, there am I in the midst of them' [*Matt.* 18:20] and 'I will manifest myself unto him [i.e. the believer]' [*John* 14:21].

It sometimes happens that the Lord gives a great sense of his presence to his people in their gatherings for fellowship. Believers' hearts 'burn within' them [*Luke* 24:32] on such occasions, their souls are chastened and their spirits feel the weight of earthly things lifted away for a time. No doubt if we were holier and more prayerful we should enjoy more frequent visitations of Christ in this felt manner, as he 'standeth behind our wall' and 'looketh forth at the windows, showing himself through the lattice' [*Song of Sol.* 2:9].

There is an aspect of our theme, however, which defies analysis and must be referred to the sovereign wisdom of God as he oversees the lives of his own people. It is this mysterious fact that God gives *special friendship* in grace to his people on earth. Such a friendship was that of David and Jonathan. It was beautifully put by David in the words: 'thy love to me was wonderful, passing the love of women' [*2 Sam.* 1:26]. This text proves that the attachment was the spiritual bond of regenerate love, for it is the nature of spiritual love to be stronger than the attachment of graceless affection. Both David and Jonathan loved the Lord very greatly and the Lord gave them a holy friendship in grace which was especially precious.

It is a thing much to be desired that God would give us in this world such friendships among those who fear his Name. They are a source of great strength to believers and they go a long way to counterbalancing the loneliness of the pilgrim way. Perhaps we do not always remember as we should what is said of Mordecai, that he was 'accepted of the multitude of his brethren, seeking the wealth of his people, and speaking peace to all his seed' [*Esther* 10:3]. Such an example is the ideal, if we desire to promote true Christian fellowship in all our churches.

22

The Supreme Grace of Christian Love

No passage of the Bible is more familiar than 1 Corinthians 13. It is a masterpiece of religious prose, justly celebrated by believer and unbeliever alike as a model of fine expression. The theme of the chapter is Christian love, its characteristics, superiority and permanence. Where in all the realm of literature could one find such profound thought so elegantly expressed? Its beguiling simplicity bears the hallmark of genius and of inspiration.

It must come, therefore, as something of a shock to discover that this often-recited chapter announces a religious principle which condemns almost the whole world: 'Though I speak with the tongues of men and of angels, and have not charity [love], I am become as sounding brass, or a tinkling cymbal'... [*1 Cor.* 13:1]. The passage proceeds to enumerate various impressive religious attainments: ecstatic use of the tongue, knowledge of deep mysteries, faith which moves mountains, self-sacrificing charity to the poor and the excruciating pains of martyrdom [vv.1-2]. It is an awe-inspiring list of soaring qualities which many would associate only with the very great and the very good. The majority of professing Christians lay no claim to these impressive achievements. But the apostle, be it said, only brings in this catalogue of excellences in order to tell us that of themselves they are of no value! This he does with so arresting a figure of speech that it has become proverbial: 'I am become as sounding brass, or a tinkling cymbal' [v.1]. We may possess all of these spectacular gifts and yet be worthless.

In these familiar words we possess one of the most central principles of the Christian faith. It is this. No religious act is of any value in God's sight if it does not accompany and flow from Christian love. The apostle's meaning can only be that the quality of religious actions is derived principally from the *motive* by which they are done. This is a truth to which all but Utilitarian philosophers pay lip-service. But men seldom ponder it seriously. If the implications of this one principle were consistently thought through, they would have a momentous effect upon us all.

At the very heart of the principle here enunciated by Paul must lie the necessity for the new birth. Invisible as this doctrine is at first sight, it becomes clear after a little reflection that Paul is virtually saying what our Lord himself declares to Nicodemus: 'Ye must be born again' [*John* 3:7]. No religious service is of value in God's sight if it does not spring from love. 'The flesh profiteth nothing' [*John* 6:63]. But love is a fruit of regeneration. Where there is no regeneration, there may be the sensational and the spectacular. But the spectacular is not that which God takes pleasure in. Before any activity of man can become acceptable to God, it must be performed out of a motive of love. Such a motive cannot exist before the new birth has taken place. The conclusion is inescapable. What is done in God's Name before regeneration is spiritually valueless.

To state matters in this way clears our vision by showing us how empty is the vaunted service of unconverted church persons. It also humbles us, because it reminds us that we are incapable in this life of evaluating any man's service for God perfectly. Many who have been famous as religious figures in history will turn out on the Last Day to have built only with 'wood, hay and stubble' [*1 Cor.* 3:12]. Others, whom we scarcely noticed on earth, will be above us in glory because they excelled us in this 'one thing needful' of love to God.

There is something in us all which is ready to overpraise the spectacular. But the quality of men's actions, Paul reminds us, is to be measured at last not by what *men* see, but by what *God* sees in them of love to himself. To remember that, is to recall our Lord's saying, 'Many that are first shall be last; and the last shall be first' [*Matt.* 19:30]. Humble service, done with much love, will receive Christ's 'Well done'. It is more precious to God than all the spectacular 'miracles' of unregenerate 'saints'.

The theological importance of Paul's words can hardly be repeated too often. All unregenerate service done for God is worthless. God has no more delight in the devout actions of graceless men than in the chiming of bells or the lighting of candles. Religious actions, though correct perhaps in their outward form, are offensive to him if they do not spring from a heart renewed by his Spirit. On the other hand, menial and everyday tasks are sanctified when God's love is in men's hearts. This is a doctrine which marks a watershed between Catholicism and true Protestantism .

There can be no doubt that the 'love' which Paul refers to here in 1 Corinthians 13 is the renewed affection of a converted man. The Greek term *agapē* does not refer to mere benevolence or humanitarian charity. It is the term distinctly used in the New Testament to refer to the sanctified affection of a redeemed sinner. Regenerate prayer or regenerate devotion may lack the external adornment of High Church ritual. But it comes up as a sweet savour unto God, who has an eye to the secret desire of the worshipper. Such acts of devotion can never be 'dead works' [*Heb.* 9:14] to him.

There is salutary correction for the regenerate man, too, in this passage of Paul. It reminds us of the need to put our *heart* into all that we do for God. It may seem surprising that a good man should need to be reminded of this. But experience shows that it is so. Since nothing is of value in God's eyes if it does not flow from love, then how much need there is for us all to correct our habitual formalism!

The problem of formalism, nominalism or religious 'coldness' is intensely serious, for the obvious reason that it springs from absence of love to God. This is nothing short of a spiritual crime. God takes special notice of the way and manner in which men think of him as they attend to his service and worship. The third commandment has particular reference to the *spirit* in which we are to act when we do anything in his Name. What we do in a spirit of 'deadness' when we pretend to wait on God is a taking of his Name in vain. The unregenerate are always guilty of this sin; and the regenerate sometimes are. No rebuke enters more into the heart of a good man than that of Christ: 'Thou hast left thy first love' [*Rev.* 2:4]. And those words were addressed to active and orthodox believers!

The reason why there is so little brotherly love among religious people is that there is so little real love of God in us. The former is the visible index of the latter. It ought to be one of our main reasons for wishing to live another day upon earth, that we have a duty to grow in love. Love, in its essence, is likeness to God. It is the contradiction of sin. A man has developed in holiness by that degree to which he has learnt to do all things on a principle of love. The best believers find their progress slow and their attainments meagre. They are constrained to bewail the inward conflict of their hearts. Our stupid opposition to holiness betrays to us that our souls have a secret unwillingness to become like God. Even years after conversion has taken place, our souls are backward and slow. Perfect love is the ideal to which believers strive. But they are humbled and tantalized by its very elusiveness. Truly, we are a 'stiffnecked people'.

Though we know so little of love in this world, yet its fruits are so sweet, even in this present life, that we can appreciate how a world of unmixed and universal love must be a heaven indeed! It was our Saviour's emphatic and almost his last command on earth to his disciples, that they should excel in the grace of love. They must endeavour to do so here and now upon earth.

Love is the only sure balsam for a church's wounds. Where love reigns among believers, sin is virtually expelled. Where each strives to love his brother as himself, to esteem his brother in honour more than himself, to put his brother up and himself down, to speak generously or not at all, to conceal pardonable faults and to draw a veil over shortcomings, what room can there be for discontent or division? Where men are 'not puffed up, do not vaunt themselves, do not behave unseemly' [*1 Cor.* 13:4, 5], what occasion for strife can possibly arise? Where believers 'believe all things, hope all things, endure all things' [v.7], how can dissension find a foothold? On the other hand, where love is absent, there is no cure possible. A church must die.

Love is the jewel among the graces of the Christian life. We know it and perpetually forget it. We see the very incarnation of God's love in the Gospel portrait of Christ. We behold him as he first washes the disciples' feet and then mounts the cross to wash their souls. But hardly has the memory of this transcendent love faded from our thoughts than we find ourselves reverting to our old habits of self-seeking and self-interest. No wonder the prophet exclaimed, 'Woe is me!' [*Isa.* 6:5] and the apostle, 'O wretched man that I am!' [*Rom.* 7:24].

Why is real Christian love so scarce in the world? It is because its cultivation requires nothing less than the *reversal* of every instinct of our fallen natures. Love is against the grain of nature. It is against every fibre of our being as sinners. But nature, in the regenerate, is under the higher power of grace. Then let every Christian take up the duty of Christian love with ten-fold seriousness. Our life's work must be to call down heaven's help upon ourselves that we may bend towards the great command to love one another. What the unregenerate cannot do, true Christians may and must. 'And now abideth faith, hope, charity, these three; but the greatest of these is charity' [*1 Cor.* 13:13].

23

When Good Men Fall

Christians cannot fall away; but they can fall far. Good men can lose great mercies through their falls. Some have lost their authority as witnesses of Christ. Some have eclipsed their reputations for ever. Some have left ugly stains on otherwise bright ministries. Noah fell through strong drink; Lot through worldliness; Moses through impatience with his congregation; Samson fell through women and David through lust; Hezekiah through arrogance; Zacharias fell through unbelief; while Peter fell through self-confidence. The list does not end there. History shows that the good and even the great are liable to sad lapses.

Few are the Christians in or out of Scripture who can stand up to a rigorous scrutiny of their personal record and still emerge with no blemish visible to the eye of their fellows. Even those who have a clean record are conscious that there were innumerable times when their foot was ready to slide and when only the mercy of the Almighty held them up. The memory of some scorching heat which was felt in time of fierce temptation is a present reality in every Christian's heart. The times when he almost made shipwreck or almost gave way to the burning suggestions of the evil one make him sweat even now at the mere recollection of them. Could Joseph ever forget the moment when he fled from Potiphar's wife? Could Peter ever again hear without anguish the cockerel's call? Or could Cranmer ever forgive the right hand that signed his recantation till he at last indignantly thrust it into the fire of martyrdom?

THE SOUL'S WORMWOOD

There is nothing half so bitter to a good man as the realization that he has brought disgrace on the Name of the Lord. That is truly the wormwood of the soul. It is as near as the believer will ever come to the miseries of hell. When a good man falls and he becomes conscious of his fall, he does not need to be scourged with the tongues of men. His own conscience will heap coals of fire on his head. Like David, he is ready to melt and to confess, 'I have sinned.' Like Uzziah, he is more than ready to hasten back from the path of disobedience since he feels in himself that he is visited with leprosy in his innermost conscience. To a good man, the rebuke of God is more dreadful than a thousand stripes. But worse still is the consciousness that he has dragged down the honour of God in the sight of his enemies. Samson's blindness was not so entire but that he could inwardly picture the malicious triumphing of the Philistines over the God of Israel. To set the record straight by rendering them a recompense was easy work for him even at the cost of his own life. 'Let me die with the Philistines' was a prayer taught by holy indignation and by jealousy for the honour of the God whose Name he had injured.

Good men who fall are in deep need of our mercy and compassion, though there must always be appropriate discipline. Good men who have defiled their garments in public are their own tormentors and they commonly do that work as thoroughly as the Inquisition ever went about it with thumb-screw or burning faggot. They cannot see their own face in the mirror without self-loathing. They cry by night and sigh by day. Their only motto now is the forlorn: 'If only'. If only time could be recalled or events effaced from one's past life forever! If only the clock could be put back or the sun made to return to that moment before the scandalous sin was committed! In the morning they say, 'Would God it were evening.' At night they toss to and fro upon their bed and wait for the dawning of the day. Like Elizabeth I of England at her end, they cry, 'Call time!'

IT NEEDS ONLY ONE FALL

To err is human. But one grave error is sufficient sometimes to humiliate a trusted servant of Christ. Though he repents he may only partly get back in this life the place he has lost. He will get it back with God. But *men* may hardly trust him any more. It is one of the wonders of the apostolic age that Peter was restored to such a place of usefulness after so great a fall as that of denying the Lord. Many men have offended in less spectacular ways and been left on the shelf of popular distrust evermore.

It was said by C. H. Spurgeon that he could write his life-story in the sky for all to read and had nothing to be ashamed of. That was a wonderful testimony and one that fully fits that good man of God. However, such life-stories are rare, even among the famous. Mercifully, Spurgeon had had a choice upbringing. It is not so easy for the believer today to keep himself spotless when there is mud continually being thrown up into his face and onto his clothes by every artifice of modern technology. Christians do not live in a thought-world which is hermetically sealed off from the rest of mankind. Nor do they wear asbestos clothing which is proof against all flame and fire.

There is only one safe course to follow and that is the unglamorous one of taking heed to the injunction 'Watch and pray'. Dull, uninventive and old-fashioned as that may read to some who name the Name of Christ in our day, this is the only sure route by which to win a blameless reputation. It probably yields less in the way of excitement or exhilaration or popular acclaim to tread in the path of self-watchfulness and self-mistrust than to walk upon the dizzy tightrope of temptation. The fruits of quiet obedience, however, are more satisfying in the end.

There is a giddy sort of Christianity in the air these days which feeds on being as like the world as it dare. Christians of this sort talk confidently about their 'liberty' and their 'freedom'. But it is to be feared that such liberty is used all too often as an occasion for the flesh. The secret drink, the stealthy romance, the private indulgence, the undisclosed attachment to some compromising idol of the heart—these are tolerated because they make one happy or as compensations for an otherwise humdrum life.

God in his mercy may give to men who indulge in such vices as these a period of time in which to repent. He commonly bears with them that they may come to a better state of mind. If they will not mend they shall feel his rod of correction. That may be nothing short of exposure to all the world. The anger of an offended Deity smokes white-hot against secret sin in the children of his own family. If space to repent is ignored, he will bring the secret scandal into public view. The feelings of the Christian will not be spared. Rebuke and chastening will break the Christian's bones. The scourge will tear the Christian's flesh. He will vomit up the dainty morsel and curse the day he rolled his sin round in his mouth.

THE ROOT WHICH FEEDS OUR MADNESS

The root of our folly and the cause of our falls is pride. 'Pride goeth before destruction and an haughty spirit before a fall' [*Prov.* 16:18]. The words come readily to mind and are as readily forgotten. Pride is a more deadly sin than man recognizes on this side of eternity. Pride is only possible to a highly developed being. It is possible only to a self-conscious creature because it is a disorder in the self-consciousness. Pride is that cancer of the soul by which the creature sees itself above its place and aspires to the place of God. It is not only the 'man of sin' who 'exalts himself above all that is called God, or that is worshipped' [*2 Thess.* 2:4]. *He* does it, no doubt, in a unique way and to a unique degree. But the sin is common to man. It was pride that cast the devil out of heaven. It was pride that excluded our first parents from paradise. Pride brought judgement on the Tower of Babel [*Gen.* 11], drew down fire on Sodom [*Gen.* 19], reduced Nebuchadnezzar to eating grass like a brute [*Dan.* 4], slew Herod and devoured him with worms [*Acts* 12]. Pride reduces kingdoms, wastes whole civilizations and will call down ultimate wrath upon all the universe.

Who, in the light of such well-known facts as these, dare make light of his own pride of heart? Every Christian knows by daily experience that pride is his constant companion. Pride is the shadow that haunts his steps and snaps at his heels. The believer who takes small account of his pride is either about to fall or, more probably, has just picked himself up from a fall already. Nowhere on earth is immune to the entrance of this pride. Not the throne. Not the prison. Not the monastery. Not the pulpit.

It is not hard to see why God hates man's pride so intensely. It is because pride in man's heart sets up a rival in the soul to God's very existence and authority. Pride knows no limit and no boundary. What but pride makes the absurd theory of mechanical evolution so palatable to man? It is thrilling to the proud heart to have a scheme by which God can be ungodded. In this way, science, which claims the modest role of handling matter to learn its nature and its laws, is now made to stand on its head and to invent a cause of the world's existence which is less than its effect! Out of nothing, something has come!

But pride can go one better still. No act of pride is more

superbly arrogant or blasphemous than the action of the Roman Catholic priesthood in the mass. The pagan worshipper who carved an idol out of wood or stone was but an infant in guilt beside the papal priesthood. They make God out of a wafer and do it devoutly in the name of the Holy Trinity! In this action the arrogance of man's heart is complete. Man commands and cries, 'Let there be God,' and there is God. Man manipulates and the Creator helplessly appears at his dictation. It is the acme of pride's long evolution that man has in this way tied his Maker down to appearing at the muttering of a religious incantation. It is all of a piece with the first lie on record, 'Ye shall be as God' [*Gen.* 3:5]. But the mass goes one better and offers to us 'Ye shall make God'. The unimaginable is now commonplace. This spirit is in every fallen soul of man and the believer is not any more immune than the rest from the disease of inordinate self-love.

THE BELIEVER'S REASSURANCE

It follows that the best and the safest course is to study humility. There ought to be nothing flashy or cock-sure in the Christian. Humility is a poor, threadbare, unpretty and unwelcome guest at the world's table. The man of God, however, ought to see that humility is the spirit of heaven itself and the mind of Christ. It is the meek whom God favours with his grace and they will be given their heart's desire. The rest he will feed with husks and not with the rich blessings of his love.

'He that is down need fear no fall,' declared Bunyan sagely. That is the golden rule. It is the believer's reassurance in times when tempted to envy the proud. All the best blessings are on the bottom shelf. The man who stoops low may be ridiculed by the worldly-wise. But the humble man will be on his feet when others are in the ditch. Then let humility be our study every day we live.

24

Christian Friendships

The Christian discovers that, while he has fellowship with all his brothers and sisters in Christ, he has special friendships with only some of them. It is not always easy to say why such friendships between some Christians develop or why potential friendships with others come to nothing. But it is a fact of observation and experience which must ultimately have its explanation in the mystery of God's providence. Fellowship in a general sense exists among all who are born of God. But that special delight which friends find in each other's company is something which goes beyond this. Fellowship is there because of the grace which is enjoyed in common. But friendships occur almost mysteriously and yet not without explanation, as we shall see. No doubt in heaven, when grace becomes glory, this imperfect state of our relationships will improve so that all will be equally the friend of each. But it is not so now and no act of will can now make it so, it would seem.

The best of God's servants have had special friends and their names are wreathed together and intertwined in the pages of Scripture. Moses and Joshua, David and Jonathan, Daniel and his friends, Peter and John, Paul and Timothy—they belonged together on earth and their names come easily to our memory in pairs or groups. Even the Lord Jesus Christ had his special relationships with his own disciples. Out of the twelve, three were specially intimate: Peter, James and John. Out of these three, one was unique. Only John was 'the disciple whom Jesus loved', in the relationship of a friend *par excellence*. It appears clear therefore that we ought not, as Christians, to be surprised to find that we have closer relations with some of God's people than with others. This must not lead us to be dismissive of brothers who are not in our intimate circle of friends. But it reassures us that there is no sin in the Christian's having closer ties with some rather than with other believers.

Christian friendships are no doubt ordained to draw forth from us the highest powers of our soul and so to lead to our greatest usefulness and sanctification. It is not hard to see how this comes about. Most friendships, if not all, consist of a bond of affection between one who is more talented, or else more spiritually advanced, and another who is less so. Within this relationship there is a mutually felt, even if tacit, recognition of the need for grace and forbearance. The gifted brother must show his brotherliness by generous, but concealed, condescension, and the less-gifted brother must advance the friendship by mortifying his envy. Thus pride is weakened in the one and jealousy in the other. Both are strengthened in their graces and as a result 'iron sharpeneth iron'.

It belongs to the genius of our friendships that we must accept our brothers and sisters for what they are and extend affection to them accordingly. The gifted brother who cannot bear to be anything other than idolized will have admirers but not friends. There is a significant difference. An admirer loves us for the sake of our talents; a friend loves us for our own sake. Friendship is far more beneficial to us than admiration because it makes sanctifying demands upon our character. Those gifted brothers who want only our admiration seek only additional fuel for their own self-love. But genuine friendship leads to the destruction of self-love because it forgets itself in a sincere desire to do good to the other person.

To accept our brothers and sisters for what they are, within the bond of Christian friendship, is to leave them room to think and act as they wish, provided they keep within scriptural bounds. This is far from easy because we are all inclined to hold our opinions in lesser matters rather too strongly and, given opportunity, we tend to squeeze others into our own mould even in matters indifferent. It is notoriously easier to quote the dictum than to act according to it in our friendships: 'In things essential, unity; in non-essentials, liberty; in all things, charity.'

Friendship is good and necessary for us just as, in most cases, marriage is necessary. It corrects our angularity and rubs off our corners. The recluse is the first to fall into eccentricities. The more we are with ourselves the more we become like ourselves. It is only when we come back into the circle of our godly friends once again that we realize how awkward, or else opinionated, we have become as Christians. We all go astray 'like sheep', but we go astray less if we keep within the flock and refuse the temptation to wander off into solitary pastures where we are all on our own. This fact alone should have been enough to warn the early Christian ascetics against the monastic cell. But history shows that it was not. The monk's cell was the ideal situation for the development of quirks and crankish habits of spiritual character. Healthy Christian character, which is full-orbed, well-rounded and rich in good fruits can best be formed within the circle of sanctified friendships.

It is a common proverb that 'a man is known by his friends'. This is not surprising because, as the Romans put it, 'a friend is a second self'. That is to say, our intimate friends are what they are to us because they are essentially like us in all that is morally important. We choose our friends, not by accident, but because their souls mirror ours and their minds vibrate in harmony with ours. Friendship begins as soon as this mutual harmony of hearts is felt, and it ends when the harmony ends. We can be respectful to believers with whom we feel we have little in common, but it is emotionally impossible for us to count them among our intimate friends.

Our best friends are those whose company most makes us afraid to sin. These friends are rare and to be valued like solid gold. It is clear that this was the effect which M'Cheyne had upon Andrew Bonar. Bonar could never be the same once he met M'Cheyne. All his life, and on anniversary occasions especially, he remembered that saintly friend whose presence made God more real and therefore sin more foul. Those who have seraphic friends will at last become angelic. It is one reason why we should aim more at godliness. An exemplary life may do as much good as a lifetime of sermons. There are some Christians who impress us by their talents. But there are also others whose awesome holiness makes us afraid. If we find one friend of this kind, we shall do well to cherish his friendship for life.

It is marvellous how different the effect of different men is upon our spirit. Some men's company shuts our mouth and seals our lips as if we were imprisoned. Other believers unlock our tongue and draw forth the secrets of our heart so that we can tell them all our thoughts and trust them with all our secrets. Some men cow and intimidate us so that we put up a wall of defence around our real thoughts till they are gone. Others win their way to our affections at once, and melt our reserve, so that we can share our choicest meditations with them. Some men bring out the best in us, and some bring out the worst. It is hard to say how all this works. But it is a fact of life. In this writer's opinion, we should take seriously our instinctive reactions to different men and not say more to anyone than we feel convinced would be wise and well-taken. When you meet a man who is not your friend, and who refuses to become your friend, you will not please him 'whether you rage or laugh' [*Prov.* 29: 9]. Therefore it is best to keep the secrets of your heart where they are, safely under lock and key.

A Christian ought to prize his friends and to preserve them. Much is owed to true friends. They impose duties and obligations on us which are not to be neglected, even when life is full of business. Church work can sometimes make us too dogmatic in minor things and the remedy for overcertainty is to listen at times to our friends' judgment of us. The wounds of a friend are 'faithful' [*Prov.* 27:6] in that they hurt us for our good. Therefore we should not resent them.

The temptation we all have is to keep to the company of those who only admire us and never dare to stand up to us. Luther was a toweringly great man, but he would have been greater still if he had allowed Zwingli to correct his view of the Lord's Supper. It was Luther's weakness and the church's loss that he would not be moved by either the logic or the tears of his friends. Similarly, the Wesleys should have listened more to Whitefield. Edward Irving was a most brilliant speaker but he ought to have paid more attention to the frowns of Chalmers and other orthodox believers. Had he done so, or had he married differently, he would have given off more light and less smoke to the church. As it was, he felt too sure of his erratic opinions and so lost the chance of becoming a great leader of God's people.

One of the most painful parts of Christian friendship is to be honest with believers we love when we consider them to be wrong or misguided. We do not all have the moral courage to stand up to our brothers and sisters when they go off at a tangent. In this respect, we must remember how Paul faithfully 'withstood Peter to the face' [*Gal.* 2:11]. We generally prefer keeping a criminal silence to giving a well-timed rebuke. But, when we do so, we do not act as friends should. We are not to 'suffer sin in our brother' [*Lev.* 19:17]. 'Open rebuke is better than secret love' [*Prov.* 27:5]. Our perfect Lord felt no inconsistency in altering his tone of voice to Peter from 'blessed art thou' to 'get thee behind me, Satan' [*Matt.* 16:23]. The two expressions appear to have come from Christ's lips in one and the same conversation. This shows how quickly we must sometimes change our voice from praise to blame when dealing with friends in Christ whom we love.

The price of real friendship is honesty therefore. A genuine friend must at times be ready to appear cruel. But we must be cruel to be kind. However much we have to wound those we love, we know that it is the part of hatred, not love, to see our brother wander from the path unchecked. However much we love our brother, we love Jesus Christ more. 'I love Plato, but I love truth still more,' said Aristotle. This sentiment is fully consistent with the gospel and, indeed, is the very essence of gospel friendships. But such friendships are rare because we either lack the courage to correct our brothers and sisters in their crankish quirks or else we take it badly when they put their finger on our own cherished eccentricities .

A good friend can be a sublime comfort to us in hours of loneliness. And the Christian will meet many occasions of loneliness in his pilgrimage. So we shall be both better in character and lighter in heart if we allow a due place to the forming and fostering of contacts with like-minded believers in the Lord. To start the day with a short 'phone call or with a brief letter from an esteemed saint can be the difference between a day of victory and triumph, and a day of depression and temptation.

Generally speaking, when we are depressed and dejected we

should seek the remedy, not in prayer and fasting, but in fellowship and friendship. As Luther's *Letters* wisely say, we ought not to go to prayer when we are depressed, but into the company of good people. Satan is always more menacing when we meet him on our own. Depression dislocates all the parts of the soul and paralyses our creative powers. Every preacher knows that he has spent long hours preparing a sermon to no effect on one day only to complete it in no time at all the next morning, when joy has returned to his soul. Half an hour of fellowship, therefore, when the mind is dejected, will often release the springs of our creativity and cause the life-blood of Christian gladness to flow afresh in our veins. Whatever gives us a sense of well-being as Christians is good for us. High on the list of things which bring us a sense of well-being is friendship.

Perhaps we fail to notice, as we read the Bible, that the highest pattern of Christian friendship is in God himself. The manner in which the three divine persons relate to and refer to one another is the exalted outflowing always of perfect mutual love. Let us apologize for the poverty of human language when we say so, but there is in each person of the Godhead a kind of self-effacing quality. The Father's attitude to the Son is expressed in the simple words: 'This is my beloved Son, in whom I am well pleased' [*Matt.* 3:17]. The Son's love of the Father is reflected in the statement: 'My Father is greater than I' [*John* 14:28]. Similarly, the Spirit does not speak of himself but bears witness to Christ [*John* 15:26]. Yet the Son declares that blasphemy against the Son will be forgiven but not blasphemy against the Spirit [*Matt.* 12:31].

Admittedly, many comments and qualifications to what is here said would need to be added if these texts were to be fully explained. But the important and instructive fact remains that the divine persons of the Holy Trinity never refer to one another except with perfect honour, respect and love. They each delight to give to the other persons their high and honoured place. O how transcendentally perfect are these holy Three, whom we know as Father, Son and Spirit! How worthy of our imitation they are in the matter of our Christian friendships, as in all else! Sin makes men 'hateful and hating' [*Titus* 3:3] . Let us see to it that we have grace to be good friends one to another for life, or rather, for eternity.

25

The Prayer for Revival

Weakness in prayer is a feature of our times. One chief cause is no doubt the widespread neglect of Scripture. For all our modern privileges of books, prosperity and education our prayers fall conspicuously short of biblical standards, not merely in point of utterance but of urgency. Admittedly one can only judge of prayers offered in public. It is our hope that we are better in secret. But who among us would claim to be free from the conviction that, whatever our attainments in other directions, we are much below a scriptural standard and quality of prayer?

This poverty in prayer is seen to be all the more serious when we ponder how alarming are the times in which we live. For although by his providences and judgements God is calling to us as his people to be mighty in prayer, we must acknowledge ourselves guilty of such a prayerlessness as that portrayed by the dread words of Isaiah: 'Yea, truth faileth; and he that departeth from evil maketh himself a prey: and the Lord saw it, and it displeased him that there was no judgment. And he saw that there was no man, and wondered that there was no intercessor' [*Isa.* 59:15, 16]. We are surely guilty at this present time of not stirring ourselves up to do the part of the intercessor so that fallen truth may be raised again in power. And it might well be one of our fears that to God's displeasure at the loss of judgement and justice in the land he may be adding a holy wonder and amazement at our slackness in prayer.

The supreme prayer needed by the church in our land is for revival. Only Holy Scripture, read in the realistic light of our modern sinful world, can train us up to pray with a biblical standard of spirituality and importunity for the revival we so greatly need. We need to enter personally, mightily, and with profound feeling into the Scriptures so that our souls may become imbued to their depths with the power of those arguments in prayer with which the Scriptures abound. For the Spirit of God eternally foresaw what frequent and sad declensions would come upon the church and in his mercy he caused the Scriptures to be sprinkled with arguments clothed in language appropriate for us as the covenant people, so that we might learn to fill our mouths with those arguments at the throne of grace.

In the Book of Psalms, particularly, we find a great many of these biblical sighs and cries for revival. Occasionally they are very brief; sometimes more elaborate and developed: 'Oh that the salvation of Israel were come out of Zion'; 'Save, Lord; let the King hear us when we call'; 'Be thou exalted, Lord, in thine own strength'; 'Gird thy sword upon thy thigh, O most mighty, with thy glory and thy majesty'; 'Make us glad according to the days wherein thou hast afflicted us, and the years wherein we have seen evil.' Such language reflects on the recurring need for revival in the church in all ages. And no doubt it is to the church's considerable loss that congregational psalm singing is nowadays at a low ebb. Were we as churches more familiar with this divinely inspired manual of praise there is little doubt that the psalmists' yearnings for awakening would be more a part of the warp and woof of our souls.

However, in addition to these more brief cries for revival

found in several of the psalms, it appears that others have this prayer for revival as their chief and all-embracing theme. So it appears to be with the forty-fourth psalm, where the arguments heaped up at God's throne reach a crescendo with the burning and yearning entreaty: 'Awake, why sleepest thou, O Lord? arise, cast us not off for ever. Wherefore hidest thou thy face, and forgettest our affliction and our oppression? For our soul is bowed down to the dust: our belly cleaveth unto the earth. Arise for our help, and redeem us for thy mercies' sake.'

Different psalmists give us whole compositions entirely devoted to this topic of revival. David in Psalm 60 and Asaph in Psalm 74 teach us by their inspired utterances how to lay plea upon plea, argument upon argument before God in the confident hope of receiving an abundant answer. However it is in Psalm 89, in the sublimity and grandeur of Ethan's God-breathed words, that we have perhaps the most extensive and elaborately-argued prayer for revival found in the psalms. It is a prayer the length and breadth of which we might well study for ourselves in the context of our present sad condition as the holy people. What follows is but a suggested outline for such a study.

Psalm 89 might be entitled 'God's Covenant and Apparent Breach of Promise'. It is capable of a fourfold division:
1. God's Mercy to the Church is shown in a Covenant [vv. 1-4].
2. How this Covenant Affects the Elect [vv. 5-18].
3. The Terms of this Covenant [vv. 19-37].
4. Pleadings because of God's Apparent Breach of Promise [vv. 38-52].

1. *God's Mercy to the Church is Shown in a Covenant* [vv. 1-4].
'David' is typical of Christ and his 'seed' are the children whom God has by sovereign grace given him from everlasting. The psalm opens with praise, teaching us that all our crying to God,

even when we are heavily burdened for his cause, should be prefaced by an adoring appreciation of his truth and faithfulness. He has not chastened us more than our sins deserve. The man who prays here is orthodox. There is no colour here for the notion of a prayer for revival coupled with ignorance of sound doctrine. His first words reveal at least the following doctrinal apprehensions: [1] There have been eternal transactions between the Father and the Son to save the church; [2] Christ's spiritual kingship is perpetual; [3] The attributes of God are involved in making good his covenant promises to the church.

2. *How this Covenant Affects the Elect* [vv. 5-18].

In order to stir ourselves up to cry powerfully to God for revival we need to be moved, as the psalmist is here moved, with ecstatic wonder and triumphant exultation in the limitless power and faithfulness of God. All his attributes are engaged to do good to his church. His sovereignty over the nations, which rage like the waves of the sea, is absolute. He is the monarch of all the earth, of whom and through whom and to whom are all things. Moreover when he overthrew the Egyptians [Rahab] at the Red Sea, the people of the covenant received a perpetual memorial to the doctrine that all his redemptive acts in history are grounded in an eternal and infallible purpose of mercy toward his church. For the covenantal engagements of the Lord to his people constitute him to be their constant benefactor and Saviour and, at the same time, the enemy of their enemies. Hence his mighty arm and strong hand are matters of jubilation to them since they are his in the covenant, the blessed people who have heard his effectual call and enjoy him as the glory of their strength.

3. *The Terms of this Covenant* [vv. 19-37].

Now follows a list of promises made by the Father to Christ as the Head of the church, indicating the terms of that covenant between the Lord and his people in the Redeemer: [1] Christ as the Mediator has himself been the subject of election to office by the Father; [2] As the Anointed of the Lord he must have the place of pre-eminence; [3] All his enemies shall be beaten down before his face; [4] His dominion over creation shall be unlimited; [5] The Father's promises to him are to be infallibly sure; [6] Christ's people shall have eternal life; [7] The elect shall be chastened when they sin, but not allowed to fall away; [8] Christ's reign over his church shall be everlasting.

4. *Pleading because of God's Apparent Breach of Promise* [vv. 38-52].
It is in the knowledge and with an appreciation of these holy engagements on the Father's part to his beloved Son as Head of the church that Ethan now turns to pleading with God to revive his fallen cause. The final section of this psalm may be subdivided into three parts :
I. Expostulation with God [vv. 38-45].
Regard for God's glory in the earth will lead a holy soul to expostulate with God, as we see here. Such boldness, so far from being presumptuous, is our duty in dark times. It is our duty to compare what God has promised in his Word with what he is in fact doing in our days. If he is not manifestly blessing his church but rather giving her over to reproaches and to disgraceful weakness, then it is an expression of our love to him to be fired with holy boldness and to expostulate with him on the basis of his covenant pledges to us as his people. If he has infallibly declared that the gates of hell shall never prevail to destroy the church, must we not expostulate with him when he permits, as now, great inroads of the powers of darkness upon us? If God has given Christ the heathen for his inheritance, can we remain dumb in our prayer-life about the countless multitudes perishing all round

us? If the Lord has called preaching the wisdom of God and the power of God, can we dispassionately allow sermon after sermon to be preached with no appearance of that wisdom and power in our midst? If God has promised to avenge speedily his elect which cry to him day and night, should we not be exercised with deep concern that mighty answers are not sent to us?

When God's ways do not appear to match his promises, our duty is not to be inactive under the plea of his sovereignty, but to copy this psalmist in an intense intercession that this sovereign God would graciously vindicate his truth by raising up his cause. For the seeming conflict between God's promises and his providence should, by their juxtaposition, arouse in us an ecstatic frame of soul akin to indignation and laden with an intercessory prayer which much glorifies God. Such a spirit is distant by whole worlds from the attitude, certainly known in our times, of imagining things to be not so bad as they are. The psalmist makes no attempt to hide from himself that the situation in which the church of his day is placed is exceedingly bitter. Rather he stirs himself up by enumerating instance upon instance of God's wrath upon them. If we too have not the honesty and courage to do the same, our prayers for revival can never ascend from a heart burning with zeal for God's honour, and fanned to flames at the thought of his promises to us seemingly unkept.

II.   A Swift Answer Desired [vv. 46-48].
Ethan is praying for revival in the spirit of one who desires a swift answer. 'Remember how short my time is,' he pleads. Ought not the importunity of our prayer for revival to show a faith in us that God is well able to pour out his Spirit upon us in this generation, and not merely a hundred years hence? What right have we to assume that the next generation will be a fitter time for God's glory to be manifested than this present hour? Will his promises

be any stronger then than now? Alas, if the languor of our soul is proof that we have not prayed with a scriptural urgency for revival. Perhaps, instead of truly praying, we have fainted.

III. Arguments from the Covenant: Doxology [vv. 49-52].
'Lord, where are thy former lovingkindnesses, which thou swarest unto David in thy truth?' God's loving-kindnesses to the church are not purely voluntary. They are indeed gracious but not voluntary. God's mercies to worldly men are voluntary. He is laid under no obligations to do them good. But it has pleased God to lay himself under obligation to us in Christ to do us good and to bless us. Such mercy, though gracious, is, in a proper sense, a matter of necessity. For if he has sworn to do us good for Christ's sake, then he is bound by the terms of his own infallible veracity to make good his covenanted promises. Yes, it becomes us to lay him under the constraint of his own promises and to give him no rest till he has done that which he has sworn to do for us.

It is our exquisite privilege as his children in this world to plead with God boldly to vindicate his own truthfulness by blessing his church according to the terms of his own covenant promises. And all the more so, when, as at present, he is giving us to experience his breach of promise. However, in the concluding doxology, we are reminded that God's glory is above our comfort, and that it is our duty always to believe that he is good, for his mercy endures for ever.

Only when we are deeply influenced by Scripture in its power will we care for the church and cause of God to a biblical degree. And only as we feel the glory of God to be implicated in the church's declensions will we be burdened to pray in a biblical way for the reviving needed. Woe to the souls who care for anything more than God's honour! But is not God's honour bound up in the good of his church on earth? 'If I forget thee, O Jerusalem, let my right hand forget her cunning. If I do not remember thee, let my tongue cleave to the roof of my mouth: if I prefer not Jerusalem above my chief joy.' [*Ps.* 137:5, 6]. It might well be our lamentation that we have imbibed too much of this world's materialism and unbelief. What do we more need than to pore over the precious covenant promises of Holy Scripture until our souls have drunk deeply into the spirit of a biblical supernaturalism? What more than to eat and drink of heaven's biblical nourishment till our souls become vibrant with the age-old prayer for revival, and until we find grace to plead our suit acceptably at the throne of grace?

The Lord has encouraged us to hope in him still. O that he would teach us to give him no rest day or night till he rain righteousness upon us!

V

The Glory to Come

If ye then be risen with Christ,
seek those things which are above,
where Christ sitteth on the
right hand of God . . .
When Christ, who is our life,
shall appear,
then shall ye also appear
with him in glory.

Colossians 3:1, 4.

26

'Until the Day Break . . .'

It is a feature of true Christianity that it points us continually to the coming day of God. This is not because we have not work enough to do here and now on earth, but because only those whose eye is on the future can serve properly now on earth. Those who are not heavenly-minded are of little earthly good. Hence the Scriptures inform us that all great servants of God have looked fervently to the end of this age. In such a spirit Noah built an ark, Moses spurned the wealth of Egypt and Paul travelled with Christ's gospel to all corners of the Mediterranean world.

This principle has not changed in our modern age. Luther and Calvin filled Europe with their theology, Edwards beautified New England with his seraphic sermons and Spurgeon made the British Empire ring with the noble truths of the gospel because they were all men who viewed this world in the light of eternity. Until we see the affairs of today in the context of the last day, we are unfit for the service of our own generation.

It is no surprise to discover, therefore, that false religion is shortsighted and prefers to offer its followers their good things today. Satan well understands that sinners prefer their blessings now rather than tomorrow. Hence he is in the business of entertaining men with the here and now. 'A bird in the hand is worth two in the bush,' says popular sentiment. And this spirit easily creeps into the thinking of Christian people. Consequently it is a hallmark of false religion that it takes men's gaze away from the last day and fixes it on this present transitory world. The precise object to which false religion draws attention varies with the error in question. But the procedure is the same in every case. Thus, modernism sets men to work for a social and political 'kingdom', Roman Catholicism directs men's gaze to masses, popes and priests, and deviant forms of Christianity place their stress on wonders of healing, sensations and childish excitement, all of which take the eye away from the day of God to come.

On the other hand, it is noticeable that the Lord Jesus Christ places immense emphasis in his preaching on the Last Day. Scarcely anything is stressed by Christ like the importance of preparing for 'that day' and being awake at 'that hour'. Earthquakes and wars, he tells us as believers, are things to be taken in our stride. Persecutions and sufferings in this life are comparatively small matters. The convulsions of empires, the flux and flow of historical changes, the structural alterations in the fabric of this present universe—all these, he informs us, are only a prelude to the great dramatic event which we are to be concerned about. Social and political changes in history, in other words, are to be looked on only as a minor affair. What really matters is the coming great day.

This emphasis in Christ's preaching is reflected throughout all the New Testament Scriptures. Every aspect of life, say the apostles, is to be viewed from the standpoint of the day of the Lord. The whole structure of life on earth as we now know it should be looked on by us as only temporary and as soon to be abolished. This is true of the family, marriage, the State, politics, governments and the universe itself as a totality. 'It is high time to awake . . . now is our salvation nearer than when we believed. The night is far spent, the day is at hand' [*Rom.* 13:11-12]. 'The God of peace shall bruise Satan under your feet shortly' [*Rom.* 16:20]. 'The time is short . . . for the fashion of this world passeth away' [*1 Cor.* 7:29-31]. 'Then cometh the end, when he [Christ] shall have delivered up the kingdom to God . . . that God may be all in all' [*1 Cor.* 15:24-28]. 'Our conversation [citizenship] is in heaven from whence also we look for the Saviour . . . who shall . . . subdue all things . . .' [*Phil.* 3:19-20]. 'The day of the Lord so cometh as a thief in the night . . . therefore let us not sleep' [*1 Thess.* 5:2-6]. 'The Lord Jesus shall be revealed from heaven' [*2 Thess.* 1:7]. 'Yet once more I shake not the earth only, but also heaven' [*Heb.* 12:26]. 'Be patient therefore, brethren, unto the coming of the Lord . . . the coming of the Lord draweth nigh . . . behold, the judge standeth before the door' [*James* 5:7-9]. 'The heavens shall pass away with a great noise, and the elements shall melt with fervent heat, the earth also and the works that are therein shall be burned up' [*2 Pet.* 3:10]. These and similar passages, not to add almost the whole Book of Revelation, indicate to us how frequent and how emphatic was the apostles' insistence on the need to keep the future great day in mind always.

The reason why men without an eye to the day of judgement are unfit for present service is not that they lack ability perhaps, or energy, but because they lack a true sense of direction. Not to see by faith the imminence of the end is to be blind to what are the priorities of life. This is the key to explain the many sad failures of recent men of genius who have attempted to shape man's destiny.

Darwin, Marx and Freud, for example, have all had a profound effect upon the modern world. But all went wrong because they lacked a biblical habit of mind and so had little sense of the judgement to come. Consequently their achievements only led mankind astray by drawing attention away from the great goal of history to which mankind is daily moving so fast. Their models of life, of history and of the human soul were all profoundly influential—and yet basically wrong. To move the world away from God is not, therefore, service but disservice. It is not progress but lost labour. It is the tragedy of our times that most men of genius have sought to move the world in the wrong direction. And it is the unspeakable mercy of God's providence that their influence has not been more disastrous than it has.

No class of persons in this world should be more moved by the thought of the Last Day than Christians. It should be our constant topic of thought and our frequent theme in conversation. It is a theme which we ought to rehearse again and again in our minds till it shapes and moulds our entire character. For in the end nothing will matter like appearing well before the judgement seat of Christ.

What a day that will be for the ungodly! Death and the cold grave will seem more desirable to the enemies of God in that day than to look Christ in the eye. Amid the incandescent embers of a doomed universe they will put on the rags of their accursed resurrection bodies. With a terror unknown to man in all past history they will be drawn by divine power, though all unwilling, to hear the dismal record of their earthly lives read out to the assembled universe. Their own consciences will echo amen to the just sentence of God upon their lives. Everlasting anguish and pain will rise up in their consciousness as they are gathered into bundles by the angels to be burned in never dying flames of divine wrath. O how Christians ought to pity the ungodly! And how preachers should plead with them and warn them to flee to Christ for mercy!

But the Christian has other, and brighter, reasons for looking forward to the day of God. It is little wonder that the words which form the title to this chapter have been a popular text on the gravestones of the Lord's people over the centuries: 'Until the day break, and the shadows flee away, turn, my beloved, and be thou like a roe or a young hart upon the mountains of Bether' [*Song of Sol.* 2:17].

The present life is marked for the child of God as a place of darkness and shadows. He is made aware of the imperfection of all things here below. He finds the shadow of sin upon the best of men. There is scarcely a church where some shadow of error is not to be found. There is not a preacher free from the shadow of frailty. There is not a relationship without its shadow of sorrow. There is not a home without its shadow of trouble. There is not an hour of life in which the shadow of past failure or future fear has no part. If it were not for the hope of the great day soon to dawn, the believer would be on the verge of despair many a time. But the sum of all a believer's sad yesterdays is as nothing to him when he remembers the glory which is to be at the Lord's return.

What pen can describe the changes which will occur to the believer in an instant when Jesus comes again? When 'the day breaks and the shadows flee away' all a believer's sorrows will vanish forever and his soul will enter into unimaginable ecstasies. It will be a joy beyond bliss to see ourselves welcomed home by the Lord himself. O what a universe of love will be in Christ's face as he gathers his people to him as those for whom he died! What a host of emotions will crowd the breast of every saint when he sees the face of his divine Husband! Surely the emotion of the heart in that hour will demand that we must be taught the language of heaven itself, since all earthly languages are too flat and tame to tell Christ what we think of him. The heart would swell and burst for very joy if God were not then to give us a redeemed body 'raised in power' [*1 Cor.* 15:43]. But how it can be that ten thousand times ten thousand glorified saints can all at one and the same time get near enough to the Lord Jesus Christ for their full satisfaction or all fill their gaze with enough of him, let those tell us who know the unknown mysteries of God.

Until the day breaks and the shadows flee away, the believer is to pray to the Lord for his spiritual, as distinct from his physical, presence: 'Turn, my beloved . . .' The physical presence of Christ will slake our thirst for ever in glory. The spiritual presence of Christ must slake our thirst in part in this present life.

Christ's spiritual presence is not a myth or a nonentity. It is a felt reality to those who are of spiritual maturity and who have their senses exercised. Hence the prayer, 'Turn, my beloved', is equivalent to the desire that Jesus should fulfil to us personally his gracious promises: 'I will not leave you comfortless [orphans]: I will come to you' [*John* 14:18]; 'Ye see me: because I live, ye shall live also. At that day ye shall know that I am in my Father, and ye in me, and I in you' [*John* 14:19-20]; 'I will love him, and will manifest myself to him . . . my Father will love him, and we will come unto him, and make our abode with him' [*John* 14:23]; 'Peace I leave with you, my peace I give unto you: not as the world giveth, give I unto you. Let not your heart be troubled, neither let it be afraid' [*John* 14:27].

'Turn again, my beloved'! The prayer needs to be on our lips continually while we live in the shadows of this modern age, in which men have followed false lights and lost their way. It is a prayer for personal and felt communion with Christ in his glory. It is also a prayer for the church's reviving.

27

When the Trumpet Sounds

It is plainly stated in the Word of God that 'flesh and blood cannot inherit the kingdom of God' [*1 Cor.* 15:50]. This might be taken to mean that *sinful* human nature cannot enter into heaven. More probably, the meaning is that human nature as such, in its earthly state, cannot enter into heaven. Either interpretation would be true. But in the context of Paul's discussion, the probability is that he is stating that human nature in its present earthly (quite apart from its present sinful) condition is incapable of entering into the glory of the upper world. The earthly or 'earthenware' body (Paul uses a picturesque term) in which we live is fitted for earth but completely unfitted for heaven. This would be true of Adam before the Fall and is certainly not less so of mankind in its sinful state now.

This is the foundation upon which Paul here begins to build the Christian doctrine of glorification. We are apt to look at this passage of Scripture and say that the doctrine Paul is here setting forth is that of the resurrection. Admittedly, the doctrine of the resurrection is dealt with very fully in this passage. But careful examination shows that Paul's concern in this passage is not with resurrection specifically, but with the future act of glorification, taken as something wider than that.

A MIGHTY CHANGE

That this must be so is clear from the fact that Paul speaks about more than resurrection. He declares, with language that is truly lyrical: 'We shall not all sleep but we shall all be changed, in a moment, in the twinkling of an eye, at the last trumpet' [*1 Cor.* 15:51-52]. Those Christians who are still alive on the last day will not be resurrected because they will not need to be. Believers who are still alive and remain until the coming of the Lord will not, of course, require resurrection. However, what both the one and the other will certainly require is the divine act of glorification. Both living and dead will receive that. They 'will be changed'. The act of glorification, then, is what Paul is referring to here.

AN INSTANTANEOUS ACT OF GOD

Paul is emphatic that this glorious act of God will be wrought in an instant of time. It is in that respect similar to the acts of regeneration, justification and effectual calling. These too are done once and done in an instant. Sanctification, on the other hand, is a process which continues from regeneration until death. It is not an 'act' but a 'work', to use the precise terminology of the Westminster Shorter Catechism.

That the act of our future glorification will be done 'in a moment, in the twinkling of an eye' is food for thought and for wonderment. It would seem to be in this respect almost, but not entirely, without parallel. It is frequently God's way to prepare his people for the momentous changes he brings into their life. In the case of regeneration, for example, he generally induces restlessness, fear and a sense of sin before deliverance comes. It is this state of alarm which we term 'conviction' and 'compunction'. It leads the sinner to ask what he must do to be saved.

Similarly, God may often prepare his people for death by

giving them some intimation of its approach, either through deterioration in their health, or perhaps by a premonition in their mind. Many, however, are called into eternity with no prior warning beyond the general knowledge, common to men, that one day we must all die.

SURPRISE

There is reason to believe that when the trumpet sounds and the act of glorification occurs, the elect, both living and dead, will be taken by surprise. No man knows the day or the hour of the world's end. Even the angels do not know it. If angels do not know, then it is difficult to believe that the spirits of God's people in glory will know. The act of glorification will evidently come upon the whole number of God's elect (for that number will then be fully made up) as a surprise. It will be for them all, and for the angels, a sublime and an ecstatic surprise. It will represent the consummation of all their hopes and will vindicate them for all their former sufferings. They will then cry out: 'Lo, this is our God; we have waited for him, and he will save us: this is the Lord; we have waited for him, we will be glad and rejoice in his salvation' [*Isa.* 25:9].

On the other hand, that day will come upon the unbelieving part of mankind as a 'snare' [*Luke* 21:35]. When men are congratulating themselves that at last a solution to the problem of war has been found (so that they may say, 'Peace and safety') 'then will come sudden destruction upon them as travail upon a woman with child and they will by no means escape' [*1 Thess.* 5:3]. The myth will then be exploded that man's problem was merely the mundane one of war and peace. It will then, too late, dawn on the unbelieving world that they had culpably concealed man's real problem, which is his alienation from God, and not that of constant international conflict.

SCRIPTURE FULFILLED

In the day when God glorifies his people, there will be a rich fulfilment of scriptural prophecy, which now lies dormant and all but forgotten. Christ's inward and true attitude towards men will then be laid bare for all to read: 'The day of vengeance is in my heart, and the year of my redeemed is come' [*Isa.* 63:4]. He will then prepare to trample his unbelieving enemies in the winepress of wrath till his garments are all bespattered [*Isa.* 63:3], and till the blood of his foes under his stamping feet spurts forth 'even unto the horse bridles, by the space of a thousand and six hundred furlongs' [*Rev.* 14:20]. It will be terrible then for sinners to behold the 'wrath of the Lamb' against themselves. They will desire death but it will 'flee from them' [*Rev.* 9:6]. They will long for the mountains to hide them, but there will be no place found to conceal them [*Rev.* 6:16-17]. They will then be required to face those unending torments which must be the portion of all who are to be banished from the presence 'of the Lord, and from the glory of his power; when he shall come to be glorified in his saints' [*2 Thess.* 1:9-10]. In that day there will be a resurrection of the just and unjust. The latter will 'awake to shame and everlasting contempt' [*Dan.* 12:2, *John* 5:24, *Acts* 24:15]. 'Time shall be no longer' [*Rev.* 10:6] and opportunity for further repentance will be gone.

THE ASCENSION OF BELIEVERS

On the other hand, the act of glorification, which will witness the beginning of sorrows to the reprobate, will be the commencement of all joys to the Lord's people for evermore. While the wicked 'cry for sorrow of heart and howl for vexation of spirit' [*Isa.* 65:14], these shall 'sing for joy of heart'. The Lord Jesus Christ will then come 'leaping upon the mountains and skipping upon the hills' to be united in indissoluble bonds of marriage with his people [*Song of Sol.* 2:8]. The dead saints will rise in glory and the righteous who are alive at his second coming will be transfigured with a brightness which Christ will give them because they are citizens of his kingdom [*Phil.* 3:20, *Matt.* 13:43]. He will then beautify the meek with the garments of salvation and cause them to ascend into the air according to an order of precedence in which the dead will go first, to meet him publicly [*1 Thess.* 4:17] and to be comforted, rewarded and given the perfect joys of heaven forever. The living will then follow.

In the light of the above evidence, we cannot do other than look upon the act of glorification as the climax of our redemption and as the event for which heaven and earth now 'groan' [*Rom.* 8:23]. They and we, who have the firstfruits of the Spirit, long for the divinely promised moment [*1 Cor.* 15:52] when the elements shall melt, being subjected to fire, and in which the 'new heavens and new earth' will emerge [*Rom.* 8:21, *2 Pet.* 3:13].

THE NATURE OF THIS CHANGE

This change will be the greatest since the days of creation and it will be more momentous in many ways even than creation itself, because it will determine the destinies of immortal beings, while creation simply placed them on probation.

The act of glorification cannot be viewed as entirely simple but must be recognised as complex. The circumstances in which the elect of God will find themselves when it occurs require that this should be so. For one thing, the disintegrated bodies of the saints who died long before will each require to be reassembled and reorganized. Their souls, which for so long have been in the glory of the intermediate state, will need to be reunited with their bodies. They will then no longer be 'unclothed' but 'clothed upon' [*2 Cor.* 5:4]. In the case of those believers who died, the act of glorification will involve an operation of God's powers upon an element of dead material and at the same time upon the living soul. The soul will be ever after relocated in its house of clay, now glorified beyond all our powers of imagination in the resurrected body.

It must be a matter of deep comfort to all believers to realize that the death of the saints is precious to God. Our bodies are still united to Christ even in death and will be reconstituted by the act of glorification in a manner wholly beyond our ability to understand in this life. But Scripture means us to be fully persuaded of this promise: 'Thy dead men shall live, together with my dead body shall they arise. Awake and sing, ye that dwell in dust: for thy dew is as the dew of herbs, and the earth shall cast out the dead' [*Isa.* 26:19]. No wonder Christ says, 'I am the resurrection' [*John* 11:25]! The act of glorification will change the bodies and souls of *living* Christians equally, but there will be no necessity in their case to raise the body from the grave.

THE RESURRECTION BODY

In 1 Corinthians 15:42-45 Paul details four respects in which the resurrection body of the believer will be in a higher and better state than it is here.

1. *A change from corruption to incorruption*

Corruption is an aspect of our mortality. As we are presently liable to death, so are we also to decay. At death we shall part company with the body and it will be left in the grave. The worm will feed sweetly upon it and we shall say to corruption, 'Thou art my sister.' 'The worm will be spread under us and the worm will cover us' [*Job* 17:14; 24:20]. Even in this life we are subject to the law of death. We deteriorate and waste away in old age. Our strength is steadily drawn from us by the passing of the years. Our hair blossoms like the almond tree [*Eccles.* 12:5] and man goes to his 'long home' at last. Our years are three-score and ten.

Even if they are four-score it is only added 'labour and sorrow' [*Ps.* 90:10]. But after this act of glorification, all will be changed. Our body will then be rejuvenated and we shall be beyond the reach of all sickness, pain and death. We shall be clothed with incorruption and with immortality.

2. *A change from dishonour to glory*

The present state of our body is that of dishonour and shame. This may not be so apparent in youth, but it is almost universally so in old age. The physical power of man loses its beauty. Gradually it loses its natural powers and refuses to function efficiently. In old age the body may become little more than a clod or a misshaped lump of clay with almost nothing to suggest the elegance of early manhood or womanhood. The last age of man is then reached, of which Shakespeare touchingly says:

> Last scene of all,
> That ends this strange eventful history,
> Is second childishness, and mere oblivion,
> Sans teeth, sans eyes, sans taste, sans everything. [1]

Such a state of the body is termed by Paul one of 'dishonour', even when it is not so advanced as in the example above.

It is instructive to the Christian to remember that this is the New Testament way of looking at the body in this life. It is 'our present vile body', or 'body of humiliation' [*Phil.* 3:21]. Truly, 'the body is dead because of sin' [*Rom.* 8:10]. This may be thought morbid or depressing to some people. It is not really so. It is realism. To shut our eyes to our present mortal state is the height of folly. A Christian should take each day cheerfully as the gift of God and seek to glorify God each day, so that when he comes to die he may have nothing to do but die. Our hope is of a better world. Furthermore, it is possible for a Christian to be filled with

203

comfort each day in the certainty that 'whether we live or die we are the Lord's' [*Rom.* 14:8].

3. *A change from weakness to power*

This is another aspect of what we have already observed. The body is visibly weak in old age. It needs to be supported by a stick. The old riddle of the sphinx asked: 'What goes on all fours in the morning, on two legs in the afternoon and on three in the evening?' The answer of course is: Man. His body is conspicuous for its feebleness in old age and, let us not forget, is comparatively feeble even when man is in his best state.

This will be entirely changed in the day when the believer is glorified. Body and soul will then be filled with power to live eternally, without such encumbrances as illness, sleep or rest. We shall be fitted for an unending sabbath of worship. We shall have all needed power of will to do what we long to do. The absence of that power now causes us to say with Paul: 'To will is present with me; but how to perform . . . I find not' [*Rom.* 7:18]. In glory we shall will to do the will of God and we shall find strength to match up to the full measure of our desire and of our endeavour, which will then fully comply with the divine demand for perfect holiness.

In the meantime, we must glorify God with as perfect an obedience as we can. But it is at best a very imperfect thing and far below what we can wish, even in our best moods. Hence we are to mourn and lament that we are as yet 'sold under sin' [*Rom.* 7:14]. Yet we also rejoice that God will at last give us the victory through our Lord Jesus Christ [*1 Cor.* 15:57].

4. *A change from a natural to a spiritual body*

This is such a wonderful and remarkable statement that Paul adds a further comment at this point: 'There is a natural body and there is a spiritual body' [*1 Cor.* 15:44]. We must not imagine that the glorified Christian is spiritual in entirely the identical sense in which angels are 'spirits' in heaven. The angels have no bodies. The Christian in glory *will* have a body. But the body will be very different from its present state in respect of the powers it will have. In heaven, 'they neither marry, nor are given in marriage, but are as the angels of God' [*Matt.* 22:30]. We shall have a 'spiritual body'. What that spiritual body will consist of we do not yet know.

OUR PRESENT DUTY

It is typical of Paul that he does not leave the subject there but goes on to suggest some of the ways in which the theme should affect us here in this life. It ought to lead us to rejoice in God for the way we are to triumph finally and forever over death and the grave: 'O death, where is thy sting? O grave, where is thy victory?' And it ought to fortify us for present service in this world by showing us that we are soon to be rewarded for the good we do here. Consequently, we should be 'steadfast, unmoveable, always abounding in the work of the Lord, because we know that our labour is not in vain in the Lord' [*1 Cor.* 15:58].

28

Heaven – The Home of Saints

That heaven is a place is clearly taught in the Word of God. Heaven is not a mere state of existence like unconsciousness, sleep, mental delight or spiritual intoxication. The souls of believers actually do go somewhere after death. They are 'absent from the body' and 'present with the Lord' [2 Cor. 5:8]. But we know that the Lord is in a place or locality. The body of Jesus went upwards to a location described as 'the right hand of God'. The body of the Lord Jesus is not omnipresent or ubiquitous because he is incapable of being everywhere at once in his human nature, glorified though it now is. That body of Jesus is in the place where angels see it, where Jesus himself acts as the sole Mediator for his people till the end of time [Rev. 4:5, Heb. 4:14]. Therefore, if the souls of believers are said in Scripture to be 'present with the Lord' it must follow that that is a true place.

We cannot subscribe to the theory, held by some, that the souls of men are not distinct things or entities. The soul cannot be made of 'stuff' of any kind, but it is an entity just as truly as the body is. The body is material; the soul is spiritual. To suggest that what is spiritual is not a distinct entity would land us in the position of having to think of angels as nonentities, to say nothing of God himself, who is a pure spirit.

HEAVEN IS A PLACE OF HOLINESS

Nothing that defiles shall enter into it [*Rev.* 21:27]. Unpardoned sinners will never be admitted into heaven; they shall have their part in the lake of fire which is 'the second death' [*Rev.* 21:8]. Those who were merely formal Christians will knock on the door for admittance in the last day but they will find it shut against them [*Matt.* 7:23, *Luke* 13:25]. Those who imagined they would be safe to venture into heaven's company without the wedding garment of Christ's righteousness will be found out and solemnly excluded [*Matt.* 22:11-13]. Heaven will be absolutely pure and holy. All its inhabitants will be all righteous [*Isa.* 60:21]. Sin will never find an entrance there. This single great truth is a profound sermon to us all.

HEAVEN IS A PLACE OF SECURITY

There will be no element of risk or danger there. That is why the gate of that place will not be shut [*Rev.* 21:25]. There is no enemy any more either without or within. The world as we know it will be no more. The devil will be confined entirely and forever to the lake of fire. The sin which we have as believers will be eradicated from our natures at every conceivable level. There will be nothing to disquiet or ruffle the endless peace and security of the redeemed. They will be saved both 'to sin no more' and to fear no more.

Heaven's security is represented by various terms used in Scripture to depict it. It is to be a city with foundations 'whose builder and maker is God' [*Heb.* 11:10]. It is a kingdom [*Col.* 1:13]. There 'they shall not hurt nor destroy in all my holy mountain,' says God [*Isa.* 11:9]. It is a paradise, or royal garden, as this Persian word denotes [*Rev.* 2:7], a choice park far removed from the noise of war or conflict. It is 'a house not made with hands, eternal in the heavens' [*2 Cor.* 5:1]. It is, above all, the 'Father's house', in which are 'many mansions' [*John* 14:2]. And where is the power which could begin to disturb the peace of God the Father, the Almighty, the Ancient of days, the omnipotent? Or who shall disturb the comfort of his redeemed family? If sin or evil could ever enter into heaven we could never truly enjoy a moment's peace there. But God has so abounded in love towards us as Christians that we shall at last be immutably holy. Sin will be impossible to believers there. Hence, heaven cannot possibly be lost. Its security will be absolute, eternal and complete.

HEAVEN WILL BE A WORLD OF GLORY

The word 'glory' is so much associated with the notion of heaven that it is almost a synonym for it. Everything about heaven will be suffused with this supernal and lustrous quality. The information supplied by the Word of God leaves us with a very clear impression that this is to be so. When the seventy elders of Israel went up with Moses and the other leaders towards the presence of the Lord on Mount Sinai, we read that 'they saw the God of Israel: and there was under his feet as it were a paved work of a sapphire stone, and as it were the body of heaven in his clearness' [*Exod.* 24:10]. Isaiah saw the glory of the church of Christ in its perfect condition in these terms: 'Behold, I will lay thy stones with fair colours, and lay thy foundations with sapphires. And I will make thy windows of agates, and thy gates of carbuncles, and all thy borders of pleasant stones' [*Isa.* 54:11-12]. The psalmist declares that 'they shall speak of the glory of thy kingdom' [*Ps.* 145:11].

Daniel receives this vision of the upper world where God's presence is manifested: 'I beheld till the thrones were cast down, and the Ancient of days did sit, whose garment was white as snow, and the hair of his head like the pure wool: his throne was like a fiery flame, and his wheels as burning fire. A fiery stream issued and came forth before him: thousand thousands ministered unto him, and ten thousand times ten thousand stood before him: the judgment was set, and the books were opened' [*Dan.* 7:9-10]. A little later he goes on: 'I saw in the night visions, and, behold, one like the Son of man came with the clouds of heaven, and came to the Ancient of days, and they brought him near before him. And there was given him dominion, and glory, and a kingdom, that all people, nations, and languages, should serve him: his dominion is an everlasting dominion, which shall not pass away, and his kingdom that which shall not be destroyed' [*Dan.* 7:13-14]. Similarly, in their well-known visions Isaiah and Ezekiel refer to the glory and majesty of God's heavenly palace above [*Isa.* 6, *Ezek.* 1; 11:22-23].

This constant representation in the Old Testament is confirmed more vividly still by the description given in the New. Christ at his transfiguration is said to have appeared 'white and glistering in his raiment' [*Luke* 9:29]. Moses and Elijah who were then visible speaking with him also 'appeared in glory' [*Luke* 9:31]. This amazing and supernatural event was a glimpse of the glory of heaven. For a moment God lifted the veil. At once numinous awe and dread fell upon the three disciples who were present to witness this brief divine drama. When Christ returns from heaven it will be very emphatically in glory [*Matt.* 26:64]. Even now he sits in glory at the right hand of God and is the endless delight of those blessed spirits who encircle the sacred and august majesty of God and of the Lamb [*Rev.* 4-5]. When the holy Jerusalem is fully revealed as descending out of heaven from God it will appear as 'having the glory of God' [*Rev.* 21:11]. More explicitly, its glory will not be the reflection of any created luminary for 'the city had no need of the sun, neither of the moon, to shine in it: for the glory of God did lighten it, and the Lamb is the light [or lamp] thereof' [*Rev.* 21:23].

To the same effect it is further added that 'there shall be no night there; and they need no candle, neither light of the sun; for the Lord God giveth them light: and they shall reign for ever and ever' [*Rev.* 22:5]. And all this will be so because of the love of Christ towards his people, as he himself says: 'And the glory which thou gavest me I have given them' [*John* 17:22]. The term 'glory' is not to be regarded as one of brightness simply, although it very certainly includes that idea. It is suggestive also of holiness, divinity, the immanence of the supernatural. It is resplendent with sacredness and awesomeness, and with the numinous, mysterious presence of God himself. It is a quality which will render heaven exhilarating to its inhabitants and replete with interest and delight beyond what eye has seen here below or what the tongue of man could possibly express. Heaven will be a world of sanctified excitement.

A PLACE OF PERFECT FELLOWSHIP

There will be nothing lonely, impersonal or clinical about heaven. It is to be peopled by an 'innumerable multitude whom no man can number' [*Rev.* 7:9]. These are described in the same book as 'ten thousand times ten thousand and thousands of thousands' [*Rev.* 5:11]. Less literally and more symbolically the same persons are said to number 'an hundred and forty four thousand' [*Rev.* 7:4]. It is the height of absurdity to attempt a literal interpretation of this number in the way Jehovah's Witnesses do in their literature. This is not to throw light on the Scriptures but to darken them. The Revelation of the apostle John is apocalyptic in its nature and uses language frequently in a symbolic and not in a prosaic way.

Furthermore, there will be the most delightful, enriching and beneficial fellowship between the inhabitants of the heavenly kingdom when it comes in its fullness. The very best of earth's inhabitants will be there, for 'they shall bring the glory and honour of the nations into it' [*Rev.* 21:26]. The honourable of the earth shall be there for 'the kings of the earth do bring their glory and honour into it' [*Rev.* 21:24].

The union and communion of God's people in glory is foreshadowed here in this life. Here they have 'fellowship with the Father and with his Son Jesus Christ' [*1 John* 1:3] and with one another. Even here on earth this fellowship of the saints is a rich and a royal experience. They break their hearts to have to part from one another [*Acts* 20:38]. Their hearts burn within them as they talk with and about their heavenly Lord [*Luke* 24:32]. It is a constant mystery to non-Christians to see the Lord's people always so delighted with one another's company and appearing to have an endless appetite for spiritual conversation and fellowship. The secret lies in that they know Christ and share the wonder of his felt and personal dealings with their souls.

How much more will the redeemed in glory commune one with another in the upper world when all their present failings and imperfections are gone forever! There at long last, with the Lord himself and with angels will the ransomed of the Lord hold sublime converse. Each word will add to the comfort of heaven because there will be no 'idle words' there and no 'corrupting conversation'. All eyes will be directed towards the vision of the Lord Jesus Christ and the other persons of the ever-blessed Trinity. Every thought will then be captive to him. God will be in every heart, mind and imagination. All hearts will beat in a common unison. The Almighty Jehovah will be the goal of every man's aspiration and every desire for God will be reciprocated by him. A sacred fellowship will be held between God and his people which no fear of sin, Satan or death will ever mar.

A WORLD OF LOVE

It is the glory of heaven that it will be a world of love. God will then indeed 'rejoice over thee with joy; he will rest in his love, he will joy over thee with singing' [*Zeph*. 3:17]. In similar vein the people of God will experience unspeakable consolation in the enjoyment of the love of God for them. In that way the believer will know in all its fullness the meaning of such words as these: 'Fear not; for thou shalt not be ashamed: neither be thou confounded; for thou shalt not be put to shame: for thou shalt forget the shame of thy youth, and shalt not remember the reproach of thy widowhood any more. For thy Maker is thine husband; the LORD of hosts is his name; and thy Redeemer the Holy One of Israel; The God of the whole earth shall he be called. For the LORD hath called thee as a woman forsaken and grieved in spirit, and a wife of youth, when thou wast refused, saith thy God. For a small moment I have forsaken thee; but with great mercies will I gather thee. In a little wrath I hid my face from thee for a moment; but with everlasting kindness will I have mercy on thee, saith the LORD thy Redeemer' [*Isa.* 54:4-8].

The child of God will then be 'dandled upon the knees' [*Isa.* 66:12]. 'As one whom his mother comforteth, so will I comfort you,' shall the Lord say to them [*Isa.* 66:13]. Such terms of endearment will not exhaust the expression of God's love but he will further declare to his people: 'I will betroth thee unto me for ever; yea, I will betroth thee unto me in righteousness, and in judgment, and in lovingkindness, and in mercies. I will even betroth thee unto me in faithfulness: and thou shalt know the LORD' [*Hos.* 2:19-20].

In this way will the petition at the close of Christ's great high-priestly prayer be fulfilled towards his people: 'And I have declared unto them thy name, and will declare it: that the love wherewith thou hast loved me may be in them, and I in them'

[*John* 17:26]. Every motion of every heart in heaven will be animated with this love of God, a love which he has for them and which they have for him. Hence the heavenly brotherhood will be eternally capable only of a well-ordered mutual affection in which God is at long last loved with all the heart and mind and soul and strength and all others are loved equally with ourself. Love is the highest attribute of heaven because it is of the very nature of God himself, who is love [*1 John* 4:8].

Who would not pant after such a God? And who would not long to be counted worthy at last to enter such a place?

29

Heaven – A Perfect State

I t must be part of the perfection of heaven that all its inhabitants will entirely and absolutely acquiesce in the sovereign
will and good pleasure of God. That is not something which
is at all common in this life. No unbelievers do that; and few
Christians do it for very long. It is the hallmark of entire holiness
fully to delight and to acquiesce in the will of God. No Old or
New Testament saint attained to that level whilst in this life. The
Bible makes that quite clear. Only the Lord Jesus Christ did this
perfectly and absolutely. We get glimpses of this in the Gospels.
When, for instance, every nerve of his pure humanity shrank
from the cursed death of the cross, he was able to say: 'Not my
will, but thine, be done.' Still more to the point, perhaps, when
many who saw his miracles and heard his preaching continued in
unbelief, he rejoiced in spirit and said: 'I thank thee, O Father,
Lord of heaven and earth, that thou hast hid these things from
the wise and prudent, and hast revealed them unto babes; even
so, Father; for so it seemed good in thy sight' [*Luke* 10:21]. This
passage is a very important clue to the resolving of the problem
we are now confronting. It shows us that when a perfectly holy
person stands face to face with the phenomenon of God's
rejection of multitudes, there can be worship, praise and adoration—even rejoicing.

The reason for such a spirit needs to be looked at very carefully. It cannot possibly be rejoicing over the loss of immortal souls. Christ wept to behold sinners ripening for judgement [*Luke* 19:41]. But what may afford us deep sorrow from one point of view may give us real occasion for rejoicing from another. There can be little doubt that Jesus 'rejoiced' in Luke 10:21, not because of any pleasure he took in the condemnation of the lost, but because he acquiesced totally in the purpose of God by which some men are elected to salvation and glory and some are not. There are very good reasons in the immediate context of that passage which would confirm us in this understanding of the 'rejoicing' here of Jesus.

We must believe that what is possible for Jesus Christ in this world, perfect as he was, will be also possible for all his people in the world to come when they, too, will be perfect. They will so delight in the good pleasure of God that they will not be made unhappy in the least degree by the realization that not all are saved and not all are in heaven.

This is the same as saying that in heaven the redeemed will be consumed with unqualified love for God. We have some intimation of this in the Book of Revelation. For one thing, the angels rejoice to obey the will of God even though at times it requires them to blow trumpets of judgement against mankind and to empty out vials of wrath upon the world.

But more clearly still, we read that when the blood of God's servants is finally avenged and when the smoke of the eternal burning rises up, the cry is heard of 'much people in heaven saying, Alleluia! Salvation and glory and honour and power unto the Lord our God: for true and righteous are his judgments' [*Rev.* 19:1-3]. And as if to show us how right, fitting and holy all such rejoicing is going to be, the voice from the throne itself cries out: 'Praise our God, all ye his servants, and ye that fear him, both

215

small and great!' Further still, we cannot altogether deny that an element of sanctified vengeance is present in such rejoicing because the doom of this world is to be celebrated by exclamations of satisfaction that God has avenged the blood of his people at last, something which the souls under the altar long yearned for [*Rev.* 6:9]. The cry of pleasure will therefore one day finally go up from the mouths of God's people when they see Babylon cast down like a mill-stone. And this shout of triumph is something which God himself will require his people then to utter: 'Rejoice over her, thou heaven, and ye holy apostles and prophets; for God hath avenged you on her' [*Rev.* 18:20].

From such considerations as these then we may conclude that it will be possible in heaven for God's people to remain calm and untroubled at the realization that some of their close friends and family are lost in hell. Further still, it will be even possible for them to rejoice that all God's enemies (though once perhaps closely related to them while they lived upon earth) are to suffer eternal banishment from the presence of God and of all his people.

Such a spirit of rejoicing, needless to say, will be wholly free from malice of any sort. But we have materials enough in the Word of God to help us to appreciate in some degree how it will be that the blessedness of God's redeemed will not be clouded in heaven by sorrow for the lost. We might add, too, that it would not be right of us in this life to do anything other than mourn over lost sinners. So long as the day of grace is with us we must yearn over the lost souls of men and seek to pluck them as 'brands from the burning' [*Zech.* 3:2], though we must never become so unbalanced as to begin to quarrel with God if he does not give grace to all men. This is what the Arminian really does and it is his weakness to do so. There will be no such thoughts in heaven.

There is a practical aspect to the above discussion which we cannot afford to miss. It often happens that a married person who is confronted with the gospel hesitates to give himself or herself to God out of a fear that they will be separated from their partner. Indeed in a rather famous episode in church history, a certain Gothic king once refused to go to heaven when all his unbelieving ancestors were in hell. But all such hesitation to believe and be saved by Christ is misguided and ill-considered. It is countered by Christ's own words: 'He that loves father or mother more than me is not worthy of me,' and again, 'If any man come to me, and hate not his father, and mother, and wife, and children and brethren and sisters, yea, and his own life also, he cannot be my disciple' [*Matt.* 10:37, *Luke* 14:26]. If an unbelieving relative or friend ever attempts to lead us away from Christ out of human love and affection, we must say to them: 'Come to heaven with me, I beg you. But if not, I will certainly not go to hell with you.'

HELL IN SIGHT OF HEAVEN

We are at present looking at what we may call 'the dark side of heaven'. We must now look at the 'darkest' aspect of all. It is the teaching, which we believe to be scriptural, that hell and heaven will be in sight of one another.

The evidence from the Bible for this is found in the following way. First in respect of the period from death till judgement we have the story of the rich man and Lazarus [*Luke* 16:19-31]. Here we are evidently informed by Christ that the souls of the wicked and of the righteous are within sight of one another. The blessed are visible to the damned and yet they are separated from them by a 'great gulf' [*Luke* 16:26]. Since the condition of this rich man is also known to Abraham in glory it would appear that the damned are visible to the blessed, though they are separated from them by such a great divide. It is possible for someone to argue that this is only a parable and that we are not warranted to draw any firm conclusions from it. In answer to that it must be said that Christ would not teach us something misleading and, in any case, we are not told that this was a parable. It may be a statement of fact relating to two real persons who died. But in any case our expectations that heaven and hell are in sight of one another are confirmed by further evidence which points in the same direction.

In the great final passage of Isaiah we read these words: 'For as the new heavens and the new earth, which I will make, shall remain before me, saith the LORD, so shall your seed and your name remain. And it shall come to pass, that from one new moon to another, and from one sabbath to another, shall all flesh come to worship before me, saith the LORD. And they shall go forth, and look upon the carcases of the men that have transgressed against me: for their worm shall not die, neither shall their fire be quenched; and they shall be an abhorring unto all flesh' [Isa. 66:22-24]. There is no escaping the conclusion that this passage refers to the state of things in eternity and after the full course of human history in this world is over. Our reasons for believing this are suggested by the terms of Isaiah's prophecy itself and by the use made of them by New Testament writers. Peter's second epistle contains a reference to this passage in Isaiah where the apostle speaks of 'new heavens and a new earth' [2 Pet. 3:13]. This term is not referred by Peter to the present gospel age or to some millennial period during the history of mankind. It is most definitely related to the renewal of the universe after the Second Coming of Christ. Further, Christ himself refers to the above verses of Isaiah where he draws a picture of what it will be like in hell: 'where their worm dieth not and the fire is not quenched' [Mark 9:48]. Both these New Testament references make it clear that Isaiah is speaking about a state of affairs in eternity and after the end of the world.

We are now in a position to appreciate the significance of the last verse of Isaiah's prophecy: 'And they shall go forth, and look upon the carcases of the men that have transgressed against me: for their worm shall not die, neither shall their fire be quenched; and they shall be an abhorring unto all flesh' [*Isa.* 66:24]. Isaiah's words are surely meaningless if they do not teach that in heaven the redeemed will be able to see the damned in their torments. The redeemed shall see them, Isaiah declares, and there will be reaction in the redeemed in that they will 'abhor' the wicked who are so suffering.

ROBERT MURRAY M'CHEYNE'S SERMON

It cannot be denied that the doctrine we have just spoken of is very awesome and dreadful. But we must not on that account dismiss it as 'unchristian' or 'shocking'. It is our duty and our wisdom to examine the Scriptures carefully to see if these are things which God has revealed to us. If we become persuaded that they are, then we have no option but to believe them and to seek grace to acquiesce in them. There is no sense in either shutting our eyes to these things or in falling out with God because we do not like what he has told us.

No preacher was ever more sweet in his gospel presentation than Robert Murray M'Cheyne of St Peter's in Dundee. Yet M'Cheyne did not hesitate to preach this doctrine to his people.[1] M'Cheyne was preaching on Revelation 19:3 ('And again they said, Alleluia. And her smoke rose up for ever.'). He entitled the sermon, 'The Eternal Torment of the Wicked Matter of Eternal Song to the Redeemed.' In the course of his remarks, M'Cheyne argues that hell is in sight of heaven, a point he admits may be new to his hearers and which he proceeds to prove in this way:

1. From Luke 13:28 where we read: 'There shall be weeping and gnashing of teeth, when ye shall see Abraham, and Isaac, and Jacob, and all the prophets in the kingdom of God, and you yourselves thrust out.'

2. From Luke 16:22: 'The rich man also died and was buried and in hell he lifted up his eyes, being in torment, and seeth Abraham afar off, and Lazarus in his bosom.'

3. From Isaiah 66:24, the verse we have quoted and examined earlier.

4. From Revelation 14:10: 'The same shall drink of the wine of the wrath of God, which is poured out without mixture into the cup of his indignation; and he shall be tormented with fire and brimstone in the presence ... of the Lamb.'

The godly young M'Cheyne goes on to say that the righteous will have no sadness over the wicked in hell, whom they shall see from heaven. On the contrary, he argues, they 'will rejoice over' them [*Rev.* 18:20]. He then proceeds to explain that this rejoicing of the redeemed will not be because they love to see human pain or because they will see the destruction of their enemies with devilish glee. Rather, it is 'because the redeemed will have no mind but God's. They will have no joy but what the Lord has.' This is M'Cheyne's explanation of how the righteous can be perfectly happy in glory and yet see the torments of the lost who are in hell.

JONATHAN EDWARDS

The eminent Jonathan Edwards had a similar view of this subject. He has a work entitled, 'The End of the Wicked Contemplated by the Righteous or the Torment of the Wicked in Hell no Occasion for Grief to the Saints in Heaven'. It is based on the text Revelation 18:20. Edwards expands the theme by showing that 'when the saints in glory shall see the wrath of God executed on ungodly men, it will be no occasion of grief to them, but of rejoicing'. He then proceeds to show, negatively and positively 'why the sufferings of the wicked will not be a cause of grief to the righteous, but the contrary'. Among the points Edwards makes are the following. *Negatively*, it is not because the saints in heaven will be ill-disposed towards the wicked or take any pleasure in the misery of others for its own sake. *Positively*, it is because in heaven the righteous will 'love what God loves, and that only'. Hence they will realize that the wicked are unworthy of their love and pity because God himself has no love or pity for them any more. Edwards further argues that the saints in glory will rejoice over the punishment of the damned in hell also because in these they will see the justice, power and majesty of God made manifest. Further, they will rejoice because they will have 'the greatest sense of their own happiness, by seeing the contrary misery.' This in turn will give them a joyful sense of the grace and love of God to them [that is, themselves], because hereby they will see how great a benefit they have by it.'[2] In characteristically thorough fashion, Edwards then proceeds to answer the objections to this teaching and to draw warnings out of it for the unbeliever.

OTHER POSSIBLE CAUSES OF SADNESS
Having considered the above solemn questions, it remains here to take some further brief account of one or two other possible causes of sadness to the redeemed in heaven, as it might now appear to us.

1.   *The recollection of past sins*
The memory of our past sins will not cloud our joy in heaven as believers because we shall have a complete sense of assurance that they are pardoned through the death of Christ. This is very clear because we are presented with a very definite revelation of

the confidence believers have of a total and eternal pardon. The blessed in glory are thus able to sing to Christ in these verses: 'Thou hast redeemed us to God by thy blood' [*Rev.* 5:9]. On the contrary, the redeemed in glory will remember their sins as those who will never be condemned by them. Hence they will sing their song of gratitude to Christ all the more and as they do so their blessedness will be increased, not diminished. So great a Saviour we have!

2. *Those we did not like on earth*

There will be some Christians in heaven whom we did not particularly like on earth. There is no doubt that this is true. But in heaven all the imperfections which here make us unlovable and unlovely will be wholly removed. There all the redeemed will be ideal companions and utterly compatible each with the other. They will forget the differences of the past. No John Wesley will ever quarrel with his Toplady there. All denominational wrangles will be laid entirely to rest. They shall all 'see eye to eye' and be consumed with holy delight in one another's company. The motes in their eyes will be gone, and because they will 'know even as they are known' [*1 Cor.* 13:12], they will be beyond all possibility of further disagreement or disharmony.

3. *So little done for God*

There appears to us to be a possibility that our poor service to Christ here on earth will be an occasion of sorrow to us in heaven. After all, how little we serve him considering how greatly he has served us and saved us by his blood! But there will be no sorrow on this account either. It will be bliss to hear his 'Well done, good and faithful servant!' There we shall fully understand that those who laboured more abundantly than we did were moved, not by their own power, but by the secret impulse of

God's Spirit [*1 Cor.* 15:10]. Consequently, all will be content with their own measure of the gift of Christ, whether that measure be looked at as service, grace or glory.

There is, however, this much to be learned here and now: that every believer would do wisely to stir up himself or herself to serve Christ as fully as possible.

30

The Happiness of Heaven

There is a sense in which the happiness of heaven is beyond our present knowledge. Paul says, 'Eye hath not seen, nor ear heard, neither have entered into the heart of man, the things which God hath prepared for them that love him' [*1 Cor.* 2:9]. This, however, cannot mean that the happiness of heaven is now in every way incomprehensible to us. On the contrary, Paul goes on to say at once: 'God hath revealed them to us by his Spirit' [10]. In any case, it is a fact that mankind in all ages has had some idea of heaven and some inkling of its nature as a place of bliss. What Paul draws attention to is that the happiness of heaven beggars all our present powers of thought or expression. The joys of heaven will be vastly greater than anything we have experienced here on earth. Whatever of ecstasy or delight we may have known in this life will be immeasurably surpassed by those of heaven.

THE ENJOYMENT OF GOD

All happiness is the enjoyment of God in one way or another. Of course, people are not aware of this. They usually look no further than the momentary sense of pleasure which they feel. But the Christian knows that 'every good gift' is from God [*James* 1:17] and that therefore we should thank God for everything. Those who do not thank God for their pleasures will one day eternally lose them. Moreover we have no right to enjoy anything which God forbids in his Word. To do so is to set out on the path which leads, not to happiness, but to disaster. Hell is that place where all pleasure is gone forever because there men are banished from God's 'presence' [2 Thess. 1:9]. And where God is not enjoyed, either directly or indirectly, nothing is enjoyed. Without God there is nothing to enjoy. The supreme excellence of the Christian's happiness in heaven will be that there at last he will enjoy God fully. On earth we at best only enjoy God in part and indirectly. We enjoy him in the 'means of grace', that is, in the Bible, sacraments and prayer, in the fellowship of his people and through books, sermons or meditation. Paul no doubt alludes to this indirectness in our present enjoyment of God by his repeated use of the term 'mirror' [2 Cor. 3:18, 1 Cor. 13:12]. The word in the Authorized Version translated 'glass' means 'mirror'. By contrast we shall enjoy God in glory 'face to face' [1 Cor. 13:12]. There we shall need 'no temple' [Rev. 21:22] and no created light of any sort [Rev. 21:23; 22:5]. We cannot now imagine what this immediate enjoyment of God will mean. It is to us a mystery. But it will constitute the essence of our happiness there.

UNLIMITED JOYS

The happiness of heaven will exceed that of earth also in that it will not fade. All our joys here are limited and fading but there they will be endless. This will be so from the altered nature of our state in glory. There will be no limit to our joy because God and Christ, who are the chief objects of delight, are persons of inexhaustible perfection and glory. To gaze upon their divine persons for a thousand ages will not exhaust our pleasure. There will be as much, and more, still to see and to ravish our hearts in God after a thousand ages as there was to start with. Here our pleasures fade as we ourselves age and decay. But where death does not exist, pleasure must go on uninterruptedly. Not only so, but our pleasures will ever widen and increase. Heaven is not a static state. What is perfect may still develop and grow. Adam, had he not fallen, would have developed to higher levels of perfection. Jesus' human nature was perfect yet he grew and developed [*Luke* 2:52]. The angels are perfect yet they are growing in the enjoyment of God as the eternal purpose unfolds before them [*Eph.* 3:10, *1 Pet.* 1:12].

The more the saints in heaven know of God, the more they will desire to know. Enlargement in their enjoyment of God will be matched by an enlargement in their capacity to know him. The pleasures of heaven are ever fresh. All the time the Christian is on earth God takes steps to limit his happiness and to put a brake on his pleasures. This is because we are now in a state of preparation and progressive sanctification. If we had too much pleasure here we should be content with our present lot. We should 'reign as kings' [*1 Cor.* 4:8] without God and should make an idol of this life. Hence he wisely and kindly puts a thorn in the nest and a crook in the lot. He skilfully breaks our foolish schemes over and over again until we learn at last to seek our true happiness only and always in him. Here on earth, God empties us out from vessel to vessel.

COMPENSATION AND REWARDS

No aspect of a believer's happiness in glory will be left out. He must be both rewarded and compensated by Christ. Compensation will be made to him for his earthly losses and crosses resulting from his faithfulness to God. The Lord Jesus Christ will not forget his sacrifices made here below. He will give to him a credit for every evil he suffered for His sake. 'Whatsoever good thing any man doeth, the same shall he receive of the Lord' [*Eph.*

6:8]. We see this principle in operation in the case of Lazarus the beggar. 'Lazarus received evil things: but now he is comforted' [*Luke* 16:25]. When Christ finally wipes all tears from off our faces he will give a full compensation to every one who suffered as a result of faithfulness to his Name. He will at that time give a full regard to every particular suffering which they underwent on earth out of the love they bore to him. There must therefore be a compensation made to each true child of the faith and it will be fittingly proportionate to their losses on earth.

In the same way there will be an exact amount of pain and torment measured out in the after-life to those who have lived for themselves. 'How much she hath glorified herself, and lived deliciously, so much torment and sorrow give her' [*Rev.* 18:7]. The wine of Christ's wrath will be mixed with just so much torment and punishment as each one of Christ's enemies in particular deserves. And so will the compensation of the saints also be. There will be a reward made to each saint for loving and faithful service to Christ while on earth. The Lord will repay every one 'according as his work shall be' [*Rev.* 22:12]. This is a powerful motive why the believer should redeem the time, deny himself and labour zealously now for Christ. It is one incentive which has always spurred on the elect to work, preach, suffer and 'die daily'. This is not to say that the Christian has no other motive than the hope of reward and compensation. Love to the person of Christ himself is the highest of all motives. There are many good things done on earth by the Lord's people which they were ignorant of during their lifetime. This is most clearly taught in the passage found in Matthew 25:31-46. However, it is not wrong for a person to serve Christ in the hope of reward. On the contrary, he himself says, 'Lay up for yourselves treasures in heaven' [*Matt.* 6:20].

TRIUMPH AND VICTORY

The happiness which the Lord's people are to enter at last is one in which every element of joy will be present. No small aspect of it will be their sense of triumph. They will 'overcome by the blood of the Lamb, and by the word of their testimony' [*Rev.* 12:11]. They will be 'more than conquerors through him that loved' them [*Rom.* 8:37]. The end of the world will come as a turning of the tables on the powers of darkness. The values which have generally prevailed all through this world's history will be dramatically reversed in a moment of time at Christ's Second Coming.

Until that hour the general sentiment of mankind will have been: 'Up with pleasure; down with faith! Up with the world; down with God! Up with the scoffer; down with the preacher! Up with the flesh; down with the Spirit!' If men do not always put their thoughts into words so explicitly as this, it is not because these are not their true thoughts. Men have always loved 'darkness rather than light, because their deeds are evil' [*John* 3:19]. The patience and the faith of God's saints has in all ages been sorely exercised. They know God to be pure, holy and just; and yet they see him bafflingly silent in evil times. Scarcely one of the Lord's people has ever lived who did not marvel at the prosperity of the wicked. It is an enigma.

That is not the worst of it. The righteous are often reckoned by this world as the 'offscouring' of society. They are mocked, ignored, shunned, caricatured, bated and hated. In many ages they are physically persecuted. In all ages more or less, they are 'counted as sheep for the slaughter' [*Ps.* 44:22, *Rom.* 8:36]. That is a fact of history and experience. All this is to change when Christ returns. The values which Christless men now hold dear are to collapse at a stroke. This present world with its emporium of vice and its huge network of secularism will be made desolate 'in one hour' [*Rev.* 18:19]. The unhappy devotees of this life's pleasures will then 'cast dust on their heads' with 'weeping and wailing'. The axle of the earth will come suddenly to a halt and the hinges of our universe will stiffen into rigidity at Christ's appearing. God will remember all earth's iniquities in that hour and the world's plagues will come upon her 'in one day' [*Rev.* 18:8]. That is the moment ordained by God for the final triumph of good over evil. Till that day his patience and forbearance will often look to men like ignorance and indifference on his part. But the believer knows that 'the Lord is not slack concerning his promise' [*2 Pet.* 3:9].

It is impossible to express what alteration of feeling and opinion there will be in that great day. Too late the world will by one means or another attempt to remedy their desperate situation. Some will seek refuge under the mountains [*Rev.* 6:16]. Others will attempt to brazen it out with Christ by a pretence of love, saying, 'Lord, Lord' [*Matt.* 7:22]. But every refuge will fail them.

The Christian will then rejoice [*Rev.* 18:20]. The age-long sufferings of the church of Christ will be vindicated now at last. Triumph and conquest are theirs. All their enemies will see their victory. Aware now that they have lived for a lie and striven only for the wind, Christless men and women will watch in horror as glory, honour and immortality are conferred on the church. In one glad hour the church militant will become the church triumphant. Faith is to be publicly vindicated. Till then believers must 'give place to wrath' [*Rom.* 12:19].

GOD GLORIFIED IN ALL HIS PEOPLE

The pinnacle of our happiness in heaven will be that it is fully consistent with the glory of God. God will be glorified fully and perfectly in the eternal state. That is what he intended above all other aims when he created the world at first. All three persons of the Holy Trinity will be fully glorified. All the attributes of God will be glorified fully. All God's secret purposes for the temporal history of this created world will then be exhausted, the prophecies of Scripture will be fulfilled and all promises by God will be made good. The history of the world is like some grand symphony where themes are suspended and discords are heard for a while. But the day of judgement will bring in the last mighty chord in which all clashing conflict is forever resolved and every disharmony is laid to rest.

So the eternal state of heaven for the Lord's people will be a state of peace, harmony and quietness after their earthly strife and suffering. In this God will be glorified and they will enter into the happiness associated with that glory. They will enter into the joy of their Lord [*Matt.* 25:21]. It is mutual joy for Christ and his people. They are glorified in him and he in them. The saints will want no joy but what is to the Lord's glory. This is what constitutes the quintessence of their happiness. It will be a happiness which exalts and magnifies God in every way. Hence God will then be 'all in all' [*1 Cor.* 15:28].

Notes

Chapter 3   The Still Small Voice

1.   B.B. Warfield, *Faith and Life*, Edinburgh, Banner of Truth Trust, 1990, pp. 1-13.

Chapter 5   The Interpretation of Providence in History

1.   Benjamin Wirt Farley, *The Providence of God*, Grand Rapids, Michigan, Baker Book House, 1988.
2.   Alan P.F. Sell, *Defending and Declaring the Faith*, Paternoster, 1987, with a foreword by Professor J.B. Torrance.
3.   David Bebbington, *Patterns in History*, Leicester, IVP, 1979.
4.   A. Toynbee, *A Study of History*, one-volume edition, Oxford, Oxford University Press, 1972, p.487.
5.   Ibid., pp. 495-6.
6.   Stewart Deuchar, *The New History: A Critique*, p. 3. Obtainable from: The Campaign for Real Education, 18 Westlands Grove, Stockton Lane, York YO3 0EF.

Chapter 6   Our Need of Faith at This Hour

1.   In Nationwide Festival of Light's *Bulletin*, No. 4.
2.   William Bridge, *Lifting up for the Downcast*, Edinburgh, Banner of Truth Trust, 1961, p.86.
3.   *Institutes* III, 2.7.
4.   Christopher Wordsworth, *Ecclesiastical Biographies*, iii, p. 440.

Chapter 7   Christ the Lover of Our Souls

1.   James Young, *Life of John Welsh (of Ayr)*, Edinburgh, 1866, p. 405.

Chapter 13 A Time to Afflict the Soul

1. A. Moody Stuart, *The Life of John Duncan*, Edinburgh, Banner of Truth Trust, pp. 42-3.

Chapter 16 A Dose of Moral Courage

1. The reference is to the Anglican-Roman Catholic International Commission (ARCIC) which was convened in 1968 and produced reports thereafter.

Chapter 27 When the Trumpet Sounds

1. Sans: French for 'without'. Quotation from William Shakespeare, *As You Like It*, II, vii: 139.

Chapter 29 Heaven — A Perfect State

1. R.M. M'Cheyne, *A Basket of Fragments*, Tain, Ross-shire, Christian Focus Publications, pp. 162ff.
2. Jonathan Edwards, *Works*, volume II, Edinburgh, Banner of Truth Trust, 1974, pp. 207-212.

SOME OTHER
BANNER OF TRUTH
TITLES

PREACHERS WITH POWER
Four Stalwarts of the South

Douglas Kelly

Douglas Kelly here reintroduces one of the richest periods of evangelical history, spanning the years 1791-1902, and captures its ethos in the lives of four of its most influential men: *Daniel Baker*, who spent his life as a missionary and itinerant evangelist though sought by a church and two US presidents for Washington; *James Henley Thornwell*, equally able as a pastor and professor but best remembered as a preacher 'wrapt in wonder at the love, humiliation and condescension of the Trinity'; *Benjamin M. Palmer*, who, in the words of a Jewish rabbi, 'got the heart as well as the ear of New Orleans'; and *John L. Girardeau*, 'the Spurgeon of America', who was so remarkably used among the black people of South Carolina.

In addition to these moving lives, Dr Kelly gives us many illuminating sidelights on Christians of the South, such as those of the Midway Church, Georgia, for whom 'religion was a matter of their brightest hopes, their warmest feelings, their deepest convictions.'

Douglas Kelly is well-qualified to write on 'the old South'. A native of North Carolina, he is currently Professor of Theology at Reformed Theological Seminary, Jackson, Mississippi, USA.

ISBN 0 85151 628 9
224pp. Cloth-bound.

SENT BY JESUS
Some Aspects of Christian Ministry Today

D.B. Knox

Christian ministers no longer have a recognised role in society; churches are no longer the influence they once were; preaching is at a discount. In many denominations and groups, new strategies have replaced the old verities of the faith of the gospel. What is the way ahead?

Dr D.Broughton Knox calls us back to biblical foundations as the only way of gaining clarity of thought and vision. He writes in the quiet confidence that those who are 'sent by Jesus' will never lack their Master's presence, power and guidance.

Sent By Jesus will help to instil biblical sanity in discussions about the work of the Christian ministry. Even more importantly, it will bring encouragement to those who have obeyed Christ's call to serve him, wherever he sends them, whatever the cost.

D. Broughton Knox was for many years Principal of Moore Theological College, Sydney, Australia but is now serving in the newly-founded George Whitefield College in Kalk Bay, South Africa. He is the author of Not By Bread Alone, *which is also published by the Trust.*

ISBN 0 85151 625 4
96pp. Cloth-bound.

LETTERS OF HENRY VENN
With a Memoir by John Venn

Henry Venn (1724-1797), the Anglican rector of Huddersfield in Yorkshire and later of Yelling in Huntingdonshire was the author of the once well-known book *The Complete Duty of Man*. After his spiritual awakening towards the end of his years at Cambridge University, Venn served several curacies in the Church of England before being called to minister in Huddersfield in 1759. In the twelve years of his ministry there the town was transformed from its spiritual and moral darkness and multitudes were brought into the kingdom of God. Dogged by ill-health, Venn found it necessary to move south, becoming vicar of a very different parish, that of Yelling in Huntingdonshire. Here he served faithfully and fruitfully until shortly before his death in 1797.

Venn's ministry and his published writings were widely appreciated, but his richest legacy is to be found in his correspondence. These letters provide a fascinating insight into the life and times of a significant eighteenth-century evangelical minister who counted Lady Huntingdon, Fletcher of Madeley, John Newton, William Cowper and many other Christian leaders among his friends. But they also contain, on virtually every page, practical spiritual counsel of perennial wisdom applicable to a wide variety of situations.

The *Memoirs* of Henry Venn have long been unavailable and deserve to be read and appreciated by a new generation of Christians.

ISBN 0 85151 388 3
768pp. Cloth-bound.

THE BANNER OF TRUTH

Editor: Maurice Roberts

Published monthly, this magazine aims to provide a serious approach to the Christian faith by means of devotional, historical and doctrinal studies, and seeks to show how that faith relates to modern issues and attitudes. Reflecting the best of the old and the new in Reformed Christian thinking and writing, recent articles include those by Donald A. Carson, Sinclair B. Ferguson, Iain H. Murray, Robert M. M'Cheyne and C.H. Spurgeon. *The Banner of Truth* also includes widely-valued editorials by Maurice Roberts, book reviews, and the latest news from around the world on Christian issues.

A free sample issue and information on how to subscribe can be obtained from the Trust's offices.

ISSN 0408-4748

For further details and a free illustrated catalogue please write to:
THE BANNER OF TRUTH TRUST
3 Murrayfield Road, Edinburgh EH12 6EL
P.O. Box 621, Carlisle, Pennsylvania, 17013, U.S.A.